"Lively, insightful,
expect from Andre
sweep through the
SAM ALLBERRY, Assoc..... —

"Andrew Wilson is a remarkably gifted writer and Bible teacher with a solid understanding of Christian theology, and in *Gospel Stories* he repeatedly uses fascinating examples from contemporary science, business, history, cinema, and just plain ordinary life to bring the entire scope of the Bible's teaching to life in refreshing new ways."
WAYNE GRUDEM, PhD, Professor of Theology and Biblical Studies at Phoenix Seminary

"Stories are the language of humanity and the primary language of Scripture. But somewhere in our attempts to distill only the principles, we've lost the narrative art so prevalent among God's people for thousands of years. Andrew Wilson is bringing it back. With insight grounded in orthodoxy and the manner of a friend over coffee, Andrew arrests our attention and captures our imagination … Will make you fall in love with the living Word all over again."
GLENN PACKIAM, Lead Pastor of Rockharbor Church in Costa Mesa, California

"This book is the best kind of biblical theology: showing the richness, beauty and unity of the Scriptures. Andrew Wilson really believes Jesus's words 'these Scriptures testify about me' which means this book isn't afraid to take some unfamiliar parts of Scripture (as well as some familiar ones) and show their place in the Bible's rich portrait of Christ. Like a 'taster menu' in a restaurant, each chapter is rich and satisfying, worth taking time over, yet also leaves us wanting more—to go and search the Scriptures ourselves. The 26 short chapters on the Old Testament alone are worth the price of the book, and form a superb overview of this less familiar half of the Bible. This book will not just stretch our minds, but more importantly, warm our hearts. Each chapter gives a beautiful new angle onto our Savior who is 'altogether lovely', so slow down, take time, and taste and see that the Lord is good."
MATT SEARLES, author and songwriter

ANDREW WILSON

How the greatest story is richer, deeper, and more wonderful than we think

GOSPEL STORIES

10 Publishing
a division of **10** of those.com

First published in Great Britain in 2013 as *GodStories*

British Library Cataloguing in Publication Data
A record for this book is available from the British Library

ISBN: 978-1-83728-030-8

Designed by Jude May
Cover image © elapela | iStock

Printed in the UK

10Publishing, a division of 10ofthose.com
Unit C, Tomlinson Road, Leyland, PR25 2DY, England
Email: info@10ofthose.com
Website: www.10ofthose.com

1 3 5 7 10 8 6 4 2

For Judith Barnett, with thanks for all the hard work, laughter, encouragement and raspberries.

Contents

Act Three: Poets and Prophets

Act Four: Jesus and Rescue

Act Five: Restoration and Hope

Introduction

Imagine for a moment that you are in a dark room, holding a clear crystal in one hand and a torch in the other. You shine the torch through the crystal at one angle, and the stone appears to glow as the white light travels through it. Then you change the angle at which you're holding the crystal. A dazzling green appears. Then you turn it again, and you get scarlet. Then you get a rusty orange, followed by teal, followed by indigo—a multitude of colors emerge as the light refracts. Each small movement uncovers a shade you would never have noticed if you'd only looked once and then stopped. To fully appreciate the crystal in all of its splendor, you have to explore it for some time, looking at it from every conceivable angle.

The same is true of the gospel.

In a sense, the gospel is one story: the story of the life, death, resurrection, rule and return of the Lord Jesus Christ. But it's also many stories. It is the narrative of God, creation, Israel, Christ and the church. It is a tale of redemption, victory, sacrifice and substitution. It is a love story, a martial epic, a cosmic symphony, a court history, a non-linear movie, a sweeping tale of temples and kingdoms and families and gardens. If you ask people from twenty different countries to describe it, you will get twenty different ways of narrating the same events, as each cultural lens picks out a distinctive aspect of God's story across time. Each version will show you something. None will show you everything.

We need a bigger grasp of that story. It didn't start and end with Holy Week; indeed, the events of Good Friday and Easter Sunday are only "good news" because they serve as the culmination of a much larger story, with thousands of characters, numerous subplots and plenty of twists. We can see the gospel in the Garden of Eden, up the Tower of Babel, on Mounts Ararat and Sinai, in the songs of David and the proverbs of Solomon, and right the way through to the raucous roar at the end of Revelation. Each shard of gospel light brings a fresh perspective to the whole, and enlarges our vision of what God has done and who he is.

This book is an invitation to increase our appreciation and enjoyment of the good news by turning the crystal a few dozen times. It is an invitation to reflect, to marvel, to delight. It is an invitation to Gospel Stories.

ACT ONE

CREATION AND FALL

CREATION THROUGH CHRIST

For by him all things were created,
in heaven and on earth, visible
and invisible, whether thrones or
dominions or rulers or authorities—all
things were created through him and
for him. And he is before all things,
and in him all things hold together.
(Colossians 1:16-17)

Creation tells us stories about God every day, if only we have eyes to see. The heavens weave a tale about his glory, the stars tell of his sustaining power, the sun and moon write a poem about God's otherness. Human bodies speak about God's careful and wonderful design, and numerous creatures display his wisdom. From the moment Genesis announces "In the beginning, God created," the story begins.

Relative to space, earth is pretty small. The northern lights on Jupiter (which itself measures a tiny fraction of the size of any star) are bigger than our entire planet. But relative to the earth, everything we might otherwise think of as huge is actually tiny. We tend to think of mountains and ocean trenches as enormous ridges on the earth's surface, giving our planet the shape of an old cannonball, with massive bumps and craters everywhere. However, as big as these mountain ranges and ocean trenches are compared to us, they are tiny compared to the earth. In fact, relative to its size, the earth is smoother than a billiard ball, even with the Andes Mountains and the Java Trench.

But on the surface of this rather small planet, live billions of creatures which are so tiny that the vast majority of them cannot be seen with the naked eye. In the top inch of forest soil, there are three hundred and forty different animals under the area covered by my footprint. If I go for a short walk, I tread on top of hundreds of thousands of creatures, none of which I ever see. Each one lives in the care and providence of Almighty God. "Are not two sparrows sold for a penny? And not one of them will fall to the ground apart from your Father" (Matt. 10:29).

These tiny creatures form the mere tip of the iceberg. Think about cells, for example. There are over one hundred million of them in the human eye alone. Bacteria cells are so miniscule that they carpet your body at all times without you ever realizing; when you wash your hands, you scrub off around five million of them into the sink.[1] "All things were created ... whether visible or invisible."

---

1   Philip Yancey and Paul Brand, *Fearfully and Wonderfully Made* (Grand Rapids: Zondervan, 1987), pp. 18-19.

It doesn't stop there. Cells are themselves made up of even smaller entities, which we have only started to understand quite recently. The intestinal bacterium, which is small for a cell (about 0.0001cm wide), contains twenty thousand ribosomes, which are basically miniature chemical factories that produce protein molecules for the cell to use. Molecules are so small that we're required to use quite ridiculous analogies to visualize them. For instance, if you placed a water molecule next to an orange, the size difference would be similar to placing a pea next to earth. And then molecules are themselves composed of even more unimaginably small atoms.

When you get inside the atom, things become a little bit confusing, since there is quite a lot of dispute about what's in there. Chemists agree on electrons, neutrons and protons, but there appear to be even smaller particles within each of these, like leptons and quarks (as a frame of reference, a hydrogen atom is reckoned to weigh about two thousand times the mass of a lepton). While these almost infinitesimal particles are being theorized about—we have to theorize, you see, because even with electron microscopes they can't be seen—there remains huge debate about how they constitute matter at all, and what knits them together. In scientific terms, it's a mystery. But theologically, the answer is simple: "He is before all things, and in him all things hold together."

Creation points to the supremacy of Christ. "All things were created *through* him and *for* him." The heavens declare his glory, the earth his wisdom, the cell his providence and the lepton his inconceivable attention to detail. And he loves it:

...when he [Yahweh] marked out the foundations of the earth, then I [Jesus] was beside him, like a master workman ... rejoicing before him always, rejoicing in his inhabited world and delighting in the children of man. (Proverbs 8:29-31)

ii
___

THE IMAGE OF GOD

Then God said, "Let us make man in our
image, after our likeness ..." So God
created man in his own image, in the
image of God he created him; male and
female he created them.
(Genesis 1:26-27)

You are the second most sacred thing in the universe. If someone drew up a list of holiness starting with the most holy, God would be at the top, and immediately beneath him sits your name together with the twelve billion other people created in God's image over the last six thousand years. Not lions or cows, not mountain ranges or stars, and not even angels. People. You and I are completely unlike the rest of creation. We are made in the image of God.

That has lots of implications. It has implications on war and justice and abortion and sex trafficking. It has implications for worship and church and mission and art. If we rarely think about those implications, we probably haven't really grasped how utterly radical Genesis 1:27 actually is.

The most obvious thing "in his own image" means is that we *resemble* God physically. That might sound shocking to some (and very obvious to others), but it's the truth: we look like God. That's what the words "image" and "likeness" normally mean. Sometimes we think that Jesus looked like us because he was God in *our* image. But that's back to front. We look like we do because he made us in *his* image. When God takes flesh—whether as Jesus, or as the angel of Yahweh, or the commander of Yahweh's army, or whatever—he looks like a human being, complete with large brain and vertical spine and opposable thumbs.

It's not just our bodies that image God. We also have the capacity to *reason* like God, in a way quite distinct from the rest of the animal kingdom. Sure, some animals can learn from experience and solve problems, but the faculty of abstract reasoning, best demonstrated in our use of language, remains uniquely human. Consider a small child learning English. The child catches a ball, and shouts with delight, "I catched it!" She's not repeating something; no one taught her the phrase. Instead, she linked together two abstract ideas—the verb "catch" and the past tense "-ed"—and combined them. That capacity to reason is uniquely human, and is a product of being made in the image of a reasoning, thinking God.

Now move onto the next clause: "male and female he created them." God created both men and women in his image, so they could *relate* like God. Because God is three in one, he lives in community and relationship, therefore the creatures in his image do so as well. That's why God declared it a bad idea for us to be alone: he made us for relationship with other people, and without it we cannot cope (which is why solitary confinement is such a severe punishment). Note also that both men and women are equally created in the image of God. Again, this may seem obvious to us today, in a culture shaped by biblical values for hundreds of years, but it was extremely radical when Scripture was written, and it still is in much of the world. Even Plato thought that women were reincarnated men who had lived poor lives, and Aristotle maintained that women were mutilated men produced by inadequate fathers. But Scripture is emphatic: humans are made for relationship, and both men and women image God.

If you read Genesis 1:28, you'll see two more aspects of God's image-bearers. Firstly, we *reproduce* like God. Just as God loves to create new things, and to make creatures that are just like him, so we desire to do the same. Secondly, and arguably the main point of the entire passage: being made in God's image means *ruling* like God. We are like God, and God rules over all things, so it is only natural that he should delegate to us, not to lions or cows or toucans, the governance of his world: "fill the earth," "subdue it," "have dominion over every living thing." That is part of what being created in God's image means.

So that's what the image of God is all about. And actually it's where most gospel stories start. God, as we read frequently in Scripture, wanted his glory to fill the whole earth, so he made human beings in his image—creatures who resembled, reasoned, related, reproduced and ruled like him—and told them to fill the earth. But they spoiled the image of God through sin. Every aspect of the image of God in humanity, from physical wellbeing to mental processes to relationships to sex to good government, was distorted at the fall.

But the story doesn't end in tragedy. God set about the restoration of his image in people, his recovery of the way they had originally been created, so that his glory could truly fill the whole earth. In this sense, the rest of the Bible— Abraham, Moses, Israel, even Jesus—are part of this image-of-God story, the restoration of his image in us.

This restoration is important, because when people see you, they form conclusions about God. That's why people with abusive fathers struggle to conceive of God properly; God intended people to carry his image, showing the world what he is like. We stand to God rather like a photograph does to a person: helping those around us to picture someone they can't see.

You play a part in the most exciting project going on today: the restoration of the image of God in humanity. As a human being, you have value not just for what you do, but for who you are, and ultimately for who you represent—and so do the thirteen hundred people who have been born while you read this chapter. We all bear the image of God.

THE BLUEPRINT

And God blessed them. And God said
to them, "Be fruitful and multiply
and fill the earth and subdue it, and
have dominion over the fish of the sea
and over the birds of the heavens and
over every living thing that moves on
the earth."
(Genesis 1:28)

Quick question: what's the first thing God ever tells mankind to do in Scripture? Hint: it has nothing to do with avoiding apples, and if you skipped the Bible verse above, you skipped the answer. The first thing God gives people is a blessing, not a ban, with profoundly exciting and fulfilling implications. In essence: have sex, have babies, travel, explore and take charge over all you see.

Most people I know are quite into all those things, so it can come as a surprise to discover that God put those desires there in the first place. He created us with the desire to be fruitful, multiply, fill the earth and subdue it. He invented the desire to travel, control our environment, have families and have sex (check out the Song of Songs). Not only did he invent those desires, he actively encouraged us to fulfill them, and they form his blueprint for human beings.

In the last chapter we saw a very good reason for this blueprint. God wanted to fill the earth with his glory, so he made a creature that would bear his image, and then told that creature to fill the earth. The idea was, as they had sex and had babies and went to the ends of the earth, there would be billions of them, and they would take the image and glory of God with them to Patagonia and Kamchatka and Irian Jaya and Mauritania. In this way, the earth would be filled with the glory of Yahweh, just like the waters fill the sea.

Well, skeptics might say, *that plan blew up in his face.* The image of God was spoiled through sin, and people started deliberately undermining every aspect of his magnificent blueprint—abusing sex, trashing the earth, killing each other and building cities to avoid spreading out. But that reading of events fails to see the wisdom of God. He let mankind's foolishness run its course for a while, and then set about restoring the blueprint, through an idol-worshiping pagan named Abram. In several instalments starting in Genesis 12, Yahweh blessed Abram, told him he would be exceptionally fruitful, promised him uncountable children, renamed him Abraham, and said he would father many nations and bless the world. The idea was, as Abraham and his offspring had sex and babies, there would be billions of them, and they would take the image and glory of God with them to Patagonia and Kamchatka and Irian Jaya and Mauritania. Within a few hundred years, sure enough:

> ... the people of Israel were fruitful and increased greatly; they multiplied and grew exceedingly strong, so that the land [earth] was filled with them. (Exodus 1:7)

Not that it was plain sailing from this point on. Israel, like the rest of humanity, frequently lived with complete disregard for their blueprint. As the Old Testament story developed, however, rumors began circulating that the blueprint might be in for another restoration. Jewish prophets like Isaiah talked about a way of somehow possessing nations, and of being fruitful and multiplying, without having any physical offspring (see Isaiah 54:1-5 and 56:3-7). No one knew quite what that meant yet, but it sounded like the image and glory of God might reach the nations without military might. Mysterious.

Seven hundred years later, another Jewish prophet called Jesus of Nazareth brought the solution to the mystery. He never had children nor had he even been outside Israel as an adult, but he stood on a mountain in Galilee and reminded his followers of God's blueprint for humanity—to cover the earth with his glory by filling it with creatures bearing his image:

> Go therefore and make disciples of all nations, baptizing them in the name of the Father and of the Son and of the Holy Spirit, teaching them to observe all that I have commanded you. (Matthew 28:19-20)

Do you see? The blueprint hasn't changed! God remains passionately committed to seeing people carry the image and glory of God to the ends of the earth. But the blueprint is no longer just about having children (although it will include that for many people); it's about going to those already born and baptizing and teaching them. It's no longer just about filling the spaces where nobody lives; it's about filling the spaces where *everybody* lives with disciples of Jesus. In other words, the blueprint is still for human beings to reproduce themselves and travel. It's just that reproducing yourself is now called discipleship, and travel is renamed world mission.

God designed you well. So, whether you're having sex or training children or making disciples or going to unreached people, let's do it with thankfulness to the God of the blueprint. And let's do it with the same passion God has: to see the earth covered with his glory, as the waters cover the sea.

iv

———

GOD AND THE WALK

And they heard the sound of the LORD
God walking in the garden in the cool
of the day.
(Genesis 3:8)

I once heard it said that before judging anybody, you should
first walk a mile in their shoes. It makes sense. Not only will
you then have an understanding of everything they have been
through before you judge them, you will also be a mile away
from them. And you will have their shoes.

We are probably familiar with the notion that Jesus walked
a mile in our shoes. What we may not realize is that the whole
Bible, from Genesis to Revelation, is the story of a personal God
who walks among his people. Theologians call this *immanence*—
the idea that God is present among us—and it is deeply radical.
Try telling a devout Muslim that you believe God walks among
his people, and you'll get a sense of just how radical. But Scripture
puts the immanence of the walking God slap bang center.

The walk starts in the garden. After enjoying the cool shade during the hottest hours of the day, Adam and Eve would go for a walk in the late afternoon and early evening, and Yahweh would walk with them. I wonder what they talked about. In our sin-tainted world we find it hard to fully imagine this daily stroll, but the language of walking suggests a wonderful intimacy and closeness, even informality. No sin meant no barrier separating Yahweh and people.

Sadly, this state of affairs did not last forever, because on one of Yahweh's daily walks in the cool of the day, his image-bearers were not waiting for him as usual, but hiding from him. In the judgment that followed, people were banned from returning to the garden, which meant that walking with God became off-limits. But not for long. People soon realized their mistake and started calling on the name of Yahweh, and within a few generations the God of the walk was hiking with Enoch. Then came Noah, who also walked with God, followed by Abraham, who had the angel of Yahweh walk up to his tent and eat lunch. Despite sin, God still loved people, so he walked with them.

You might think that changed with the law of Moses. All those sacrifices and commandments and curtains look like they have separated people from God altogether, and it certainly doesn't seem to suggest he's walking among them. But that's exactly what he is doing: "the LORD your God walks in the midst of your camp" (Deut. 23:14). The law of Moses is a set of instructions about how people should respond to the God of the walk, not evidence that he is no longer available.

Of course, God is spirit, and so we shouldn't take every image literally. The people couldn't see God's footprints in the sand as he walked "in the midst" of their campsites. On the other hand, a wonderful passage in Daniel protects us from making the opposite mistake of dialling down the language of "walking" so much that the note of immanent presence is lost. Look:

> Then King Nebuchadnezzar was astonished and rose up in haste. He declared to his counselors, "Did we not cast three men bound into the fire?" They answered and said to the king, "True, O king." He answered and said, "But I see four men unbound, walking in the midst of the fire, and they are not hurt; and the appearance of the fourth is like a son of the gods." (Daniel 3:24-25)

With that in mind, consider Jesus. There's certainly nothing metaphorical here: Jesus literally walked many thousands of miles in humanity's shoes. In the first few months of his ministry, Luke records him walking from Nazareth to Judea to Nazareth to Capernaum to Judea to Lake Galilee to Capernaum to Nain, a distance of around 750 miles, and that's without including going "through towns and villages" (Lk. 13:22) and withdrawing "to desolate places" (Lk. 5:16). He walked up arid hills and through barren scrubland and down narrow lanes and even on water. He walked with rich and poor, famous and infamous. He walked with no bodyguards or protective cordon, sometimes alone, sometimes through streets so crowded he could hardly move. He walked up the mountain to be transfigured before Moses and Elijah, and then walked down again to be rejected by a Samaritan village so small we don't even know its name.

He wore sandals and got blisters and stepped in dung and got physically exhausted. He walked to Golgotha with a wooden stake on his back, then walked out of the tomb before walking to Emmaus. Finally, after walking out to Bethany, he ascended into heaven, walked through the holy places to the right hand of the Father, and with his mission accomplished ... he sat down.

But he's still the God of the walk. In John's vision of heaven, we find Jesus again in the midst of his churches, the "golden lampstands" (Rev. 1:12). Unlike the purposeful stride of his earthly walk, he takes a gentle amble here, a walk of friendship and fellowship, more like Eden than Galilee. After his ascension he sent his Spirit so that we could know the God of the walk with us at all times, so we could walk in him, keep in step with him, and experience his immanent presence with us wherever we go.

SHAME REMOVED

And the LORD God made for Adam
and for his wife garments of skins
and clothed them.
(Genesis 3:21)

I don't know whether you've ever had *the* dream? You know, the one where you find yourself in a public place of some sort—an office or (worse) a school—and you gradually become aware of people looking at you and pointing. You try to ignore it, but you eventually look down, and discover you are totally naked. In the corridor. The sense of shame and horror is so overwhelming that you usually wake up immediately, shuddering and breathing deeply.

No doubt psychologists have their theories about the origins of the naked dream, but the real answer dates back to Eden. In this beautiful, once-perfect garden, nakedness first became associated with that terrible phenomenon, shame. The story is so well known that we can miss it, but nakedness and shame are intertwined throughout Genesis 2–3, and they have been ever since. The parts of the body that can be displayed publicly vary enormously from culture to culture (just the eyes for Yemeni women, arms and legs in European cities, everything but the genitals in some equatorial tribes), but complete nakedness is rarely normal among adults in public. Somewhere in the human psyche a primal association exists between being naked and being ashamed.

To understand this, we need to follow the story of Adam and Eve. When God first brought Adam his bride, they "were both naked and were not ashamed" (Gen. 2:25). God created them without clothes, brought them together in the Bible's first marriage, and blessed their sexual unity as one flesh; there was nothing to hide, either physically or spiritually.

But then sin happened. By twisting and misrepresenting his words, the serpent got the woman, and then the man, to disobey God. Reading the story thousands of years later, we know the consequences: organic sin in the human race, relationship with God broken, perfect creation spoiled, gender roles distorted, and death itself entering the story. But we often miss something from the terrible fall-out list:

> Then the eyes of both were opened, and they knew that
> they were naked. And they sewed fig leaves together and
> made themselves loincloths. (Genesis 3:7)

The first consequence of sin, at least from mankind's point of view, was the shame of nakedness. As if to symbolize the terrible spiritual shame they felt for breaking God's commandment, the man and the woman felt a terrible physical shame at being unclothed. In seconds, Adam and Eve had become sinful creatures before an all-knowing and all-powerful God, and their first instinct (as in all cover-ups from Eden to Watergate) was to conceal everything, including their physical bodies. Faced with fractured relationships and the prospect of death, they responded by sewing loincloths out of fig leaves to hide their embarrassment. Their second action, trying to hide from God, was similarly motivated, and similarly futile. Nakedness and transparency, intended as blessings, had become a disgrace through the corrupting power of sin.

Only one thing in the world can overcome disgrace, and that is grace. Sin is judged and punished, of course (Gen. 3:16-19). But whereas Adam and Eve's first action was to hide their nakedness clumsily, God's first action was to hide their nakedness perfectly. Yahweh kills an animal to make them "garments of skins" and clothes them, removing the crippling dishonor they felt in their nakedness, and demonstrating that even though they were incapable of covering their shame, the living God could (Gen. 3:21).

When Scripture speaks of being clothed in garments of salvation (Is. 61:10), pure vestments (Zech. 3:4) and white linen (Rev. 19:7-8, 14), it is not just telling us of sins forgiven, as wonderful as that is—it is telling us of shame removed. Striving replaced by sacrifice, shame by shelter, disgrace by grace.

Do you see? When confronted with the presence of Yahweh, sin led to an unbearable sense of exposure and humiliation for the man and the woman. And it always does. Human attempts to cope with sin's stigma proved futile, and they always have. It took the gracious intervention of God through a blood sacrifice to remove their disgrace. And it always has.

vi

AUTHORITY REGAINED

And Jesus came and said to them, "All
authority in heaven and on earth has
been given to me. Go therefore and make
disciples of all nations, baptizing them
in the name of the Father and of the Son
and of the Holy Spirit, teaching them to
observe all that I have commanded you."
(Matthew 28:18-20)

History is about authority. It is about other things as well, but it is always about that. God's story begins and ends with authority being given. God's very first commandment to the man was that he should exercise authority over creation:

> "Be fruitful and multiply and *fill the earth* and *subdue* it, and *have dominion over* the fish of the sea and over the birds of the heavens and over every living thing that moves on the earth." (Genesis 1:28, my italics)

27

What a dramatic piece of delegation! God, who spends the first twenty-seven verses of Genesis 1 speaking space and spiders into being, immediately gives his image-bearers the responsibility of ruling over creation on his behalf. The way mankind goes on to handle this authority will affect the fruitfulness and productivity of the entire universe: just as America flourished under Franklin Roosevelt and Zimbabwe starved under Robert Mugabe, so the fate of earth sat in the hands of its delegated rulers Adam and Eve. Despite the incredible impact people's actions will have, God sees dominion over creation as an integral part of his plan for humanity, so he hands it down. And he waits.

Humankind proceeds to exercise authority more like Mugabe than Roosevelt. The man—the head of the relationship, created first and ultimately accountable for what happened—abdicates his responsibilities by allowing the serpent to tempt his wife, even though he was "with her" at the time (Gen. 3:6). The woman, in charge by default through her husband's sin, gives implicit authority to the serpent by listening to his lies instead of Yahweh. In a few verses, the created order was inverted. The results are tragic, but predictable. The land, responding to the bungled authority structure, produces thorns and thistles instead of fruitful abundance, and Satan becomes the acting ruler over the earth: the "prince of the power of the air, the spirit that is now at work in the sons of disobedience" (Eph. 2:2).

Throughout the Old Testament, of course, God remained sovereign, and we should not flatter Satan by exaggerating his authority (look at Job 1-2, for instance). But in some ways, Satan continued to hold sway over the earth for thousands of years. Because it was a man who was originally given the authority to rule, and a man who lost it, it had to be a man who regained it. And since no man was up to the job, the effective authority over the earth remained with the devil, sometimes even called "the god of this world" (2 Cor. 4:4).

Until Jesus. A number of things were at stake during his temptation in the wilderness, but perhaps the most significant was authority over the earth. Satan knew if he could just get Jesus to acknowledge *his* authority instead of God's, then it was game over. He offered Jesus all the kingdoms of the world, and all their glory, in exchange for worship. Given that the alternative option for regaining man's authority involved the cross, this must have seemed a tempting compromise. But Jesus stood firm, refusing to change the plan. In that moment, Jesus lit a timebomb set next to the devil's authority over mankind. Three years and counting.

Sure enough, right on time the bomb exploded in spectacular fashion. As Jesus prayed in Gethsemane, remained silent in the trial and endured the nails at Golgotha, the utter authority of God was never compromised: "Not my will, but yours" (Lk. 22:42). At long last a man had arisen who took seriously humanity's commission to govern the earth with God's authority, and the devil's mandate crumbled. Just as one man conceded authority to Satan, one man wrenched it back. Mankind again holds the right to rule creation, through Jesus, "the head of all rule and authority" (Col. 2:10).

When Jesus gathered his disciples on a Galilean mountain and told them, "All authority in heaven and on earth has been given to me," he meant it. He had lived a life of unswerving obedience to the will of God, had defied the devil's temptation at every step, and therefore had regained the authority once given to mankind in the garden. No more would people's dominion be shared with, or even stolen by, other creatures. Jesus, and Jesus alone, holds all authority in heaven and on earth.

THE RAINBOW

When I bring clouds over the earth and
the bow is seen in the clouds, I will
remember my covenant that is between me
and you and every living creature of all
flesh. And the waters shall never again
become a flood to destroy all flesh. When
the bow is in the clouds, I will see it
and remember the everlasting covenant
between God and every living creature of
all flesh that is on the earth.
(Genesis 9:14-16)

Promises make the world go round. Variously called con-
tracts, affirmations, oaths and vows, promises are everywhere.
Hundreds of marriages every week include words like "in
the presence of God I make this vow." Two and a half centuries ago in Philadelphia, a nation was established with "we
mutually pledge to each other our lives, our fortunes and

our sacred honor." Human interactions would be impossible without promises.

Yet of all the people who make promises every day, only God has never broken one.[1] We say that we'll be there, and we're not; we say "I do," and we don't; we tell people we won't let them down, and we do. But God goes on, making promise after promise, century after century. And keeps all of them.

One of his oldest promises takes the form of a glorious, mysterious, multicolored arc of refracted light. Rainbows have inspired a thousand sighs and a million playgroup paintings, but its first mention in recorded history formed a guarantee of God's promise. And not just any promise: it was the guarantee of a covenant, a special and one-sided, unconditional promise to never again destroy the earth by floods. Given humankind's track record at this point in the story, this was quite a remarkable commitment on God's part. But even more remarkable is that, in his interactions with humanity over the last several thousand years, he has never broken it.

If you look at the story of Noah, you will see that the rainbow, perhaps more than anything else, displays God's grace. People had sinned, committing murder and violence and polygamy and all sorts of other things. They had sinned so consistently that God regretted making them in the first place. Genesis 6:5 explains how bleak things were: "every intention of the thoughts of his [people's] heart was only evil continually." If ever there was a generation that deserved to get humanity wiped out forever, it was this one: *every* intention, *only* evil, *continually*.

---

1   I owe the following piece of phrasing to John Ortberg.

Yet God responded, again, with unmerited kindness; he destroys the wicked, as befits his justice, but slips several grace-moments into the story. First, he rescues Noah and his family. Then, as soon as they leave the ark, he announces that he will never again strike the earth and everything that lives on it (8:21). Next, he re-issues the commission he gave to Adam and Eve (9:1), gifting humanity a fresh start, and allowing them to begin filling the earth once again. Finally, he makes a covenant with Noah for all future generations, giving the rainbow as his sign. No matter what happens, God covenants not to flood the planet, and the rainbow serves as a permanent reminder.

This covenant is not a contract. A contract is a conditional arrangement: if you give me this, I'll give you that. Generally, if a contract is broken by one party, then the other is released from their obligations—"he didn't provide the paint job I wanted, so I don't have to pay him." But the rainbow-covenant is one of grace, and therefore completely one-sided. God grounds his covenant not in our commitment to be righteous, but in his commitment to be gracious. In fact, God knew that we would continue to be wicked, and he made the covenant anyway. He foresaw child sacrifice and child slavery, the Holocaust and the Gulag, adultery and abortion, genocide and rape; but his grace was so extravagant that he guaranteed never to destroy the whole earth, no matter what happened. He left the rainbow in the sky as a guarantee.

The rainbow is meant to be beautiful and eye-catching, because it's meant to draw us back to the covenant God made with Noah. Its main purpose in this story, however, is not to remind *us* of God's covenant and faithfulness, but to remind

God. Of course, in a literal sense God never forgets, but the rainbow brings his promises to mind, and whenever he sees the sky filled with an arc of light, there is a divine recommitment never again to destroy the earth. Because he said he wouldn't. Because he made a covenant.

If you are looking for evidence of the grace and faithfulness of God, I can tell you where to find it: at the end of a rainbow.

THE CITY AND THE TOWER

> Then they said, "Come, let us build
> ourselves a city and a tower with
> its top in the heavens, and let us
> make a name for ourselves, lest we be
> dispersed over the face of the whole
> earth." And the LORD came down to see
> the city and the tower, which the
> children of man had built.
> (Genesis 11:4-5)

Tell a child about the Tower of Babel, and they might well conclude that God doesn't like big buildings. If you're not careful, the story can sound like that. People get together and build a big tower; God doesn't like it; so he cancels the project by muddling up languages, and in one fell swoop produces racial conflict and Latin lessons. What is all that about?

Read carefully, however, the Babel story is a powerful statement about the sovereignty of God, the sin of man and

the supremacy of Christ. The themes and consequences of
Babel flow out through Scripture, where we see three major
reversals. Firstly, a close reading reveals the famous Tower of
Babel to be only half the story. Mankind actually decides to
build a city *and* a tower; the tower to secure fame, and the
city to avoid being "dispersed over the face of the whole
earth"—a deliberate act of defiance against the living God.
Making a name for themselves, rather than for Yahweh, is
an act of smugness at best, idolatry at worst. But building a
city to avoid being dispersed is just as bad, because they are
disobeying the original God-given commission to go forth and
multiply. Yahweh wanted his glory to fill the earth, but people
chose security instead of mission, as well as self-glory instead
of God's glory.

It's not about buildings. God loves building: he gave Noah
detailed blueprints on how to construct the most stable boat
imaginable, architectural plans take up numerous chapters
in Scripture, and the people of God are a beautiful structure
(Ezek. 40-48) and a stunning city (Rev. 21). The issue isn't
buildings—it's blasphemy. The people built the city and the
tower to oppose God. The author of Genesis cannot restrain
his sarcasm when he comments witheringly that Yahweh
"came down to see the city and the tower, which the children
of man had built." The designer of Mount Everest is unim-
pressed; he has to peer down from heaven to find out what
all the fuss is about. The confusion of language, and the
dispersal, soon follow.

As so often in Scripture, however, the rescue plan starts
almost immediately. God calls a man from the same part of
the world, an idol-worshiper whose community had the same

habit of building temples to foreign gods, and tells him to go to a new land. His name is Abram. Yahweh's call begins a remarkable reversal of Babel—Abram is to leave his land, rather than stay in his city; all the now separated nations will be blessed through him; and rather than making a name for himself, Yahweh will make a name for him. A great name is given to one who makes himself nothing, and a great city to one who leaves his home and heads off into a strange land. The pattern of the story is set.

The second great reversal of Babel occurs at Pentecost. The curse of God at Babel had the obvious effect of causing brothers to become foreigners, making people unable to understand each other, dispersing humanity and bringing God's judgment. In Acts 2, the gift of God at Pentecost does the exact opposite, causing foreigners to become brothers, allowing people to understand each other, uniting humanity and bringing God's blessing:

> And they were all filled with the Holy Spirit and began to speak in other tongues as the Spirit gave them utterance. Now there were dwelling in Jerusalem Jews, devout men from every nation under heaven. And at this sound the multitude came together, and they were bewildered, because each one was hearing them speak in his own language. (Acts 2:4-6)

Throughout the history of the church, from Corinth to Korea, the gift of speaking in tongues has served this function. I know of several who have seen conversions as they preached in Cantonese or Hindi without ever learning the language.

Every time that happens, the blessing overcomes the curse, and Babel unravels a little bit more.

The ultimate undoing of Babel, however, is still in the future. The best is yet to come. We await the day when the tower and power of Babel will be permanently destroyed, and when no one will want to make a name for themselves or build a city to avoid dispersion. On that day, there will be one name with no rivalry, one people with no racism, one city with no tower, and one cry on the lips of every person from every language and tongue:

> After this I looked, and behold, a great multitude that no one could number, from every nation, from all tribes and peoples and languages, standing before the throne and before the Lamb, clothed in white robes, with palm branches in their hands, and crying out with a loud voice, "Salvation belongs to our God who sits on the throne, and to the Lamb!" (Revelation 7:9-10)

ACT TWO

ISRAEL AND HISTORY

i
———

THE STORY BENEATH

And he said to them, "O foolish ones,
and slow of heart to believe all that
the prophets have spoken! Was it not
necessary that the Christ should
suffer these things and enter into his
glory?" And beginning with Moses and
all the Prophets, he interpreted to
them in all the Scriptures the things
concerning himself.
(Luke 24:25-27)

Throughout the Old Testament, there's a story beneath the story. Just like *spoiler alert* when you discover Brad Pitt and Edward Norton are the same person in *Fight Club*, and Bruce Willis is actually dead all along in *The Sixth Sense*. Everything that seemed to make sense has to be rethought, but when you watch the film again, the whole thing hangs together so much better, and you spot clues everywhere.

With that in mind, consider Emmaus. It's a Sunday afternoon and two companions, probably a husband and wife, trudge along the road. Like virtually all first-century Jews, they have spent their whole lives waiting for God to send someone who would deliver Israel from the hands of the Romans, and in the last few months they have come across someone who looks like he fits the bill: a prophet, mighty in word and deed, called Jesus of Nazareth. A few days ago, however, disaster had struck. Instead of Jesus destroying the Romans, the Romans destroyed Jesus and he has been dead for two days. Which means that he can't possibly have been Israel's King. Despite one or two rumors to the contrary, the narrative seems to have ended in tragedy. But things are not always what they seem …

If I had just been resurrected, I might be tempted to arrive with as much fanfare as possible. Yet Jesus doesn't do that. In fact, he doesn't even allow them to recognize him, and he spends the next hour or two explaining the bombshell, the story beneath the story, the truth that all the Scriptures pointed to, even if no one had noticed. It is simply this: "that the Christ should suffer these things and enter into his glory."

The couple on the Emmaus Road would not have summarized the Old Testament like that. Neither, presumably, would any of us if we'd been in their place. Once you know it, though, the twist is blindingly obvious. The Messiah would enter into glory through *suffering*—suddenly it's noticeable in every Old Testament book. Genesis is full of altars, where innocent animals die on behalf of people. Genesis begins and ends with righteous blood being spilt by the wicked. The law is largely comprised of detailed instructions on how people can get made right with God through substitutionary sacrifice—

the suffering of the innocent. Israel's history demonstrates how those who are faithful to God, like Moses and Samuel and Elijah, are rejected by the people and encounter great suffering for their righteousness. David enters his glory and kingship through suffering at the hands of King Saul, then gets rejected by his son, and pens suffering songs like Psalm 22. When you remember that the Christ was to be the new David, it's hard to escape the conclusion that the Christ would also "suffer these things and enter into his glory."

That's the story beneath the story. It was necessary that the Christ, the anointed one of God for whom the Jews had been waiting for centuries, would suffer death on behalf of his people and then be vindicated. So Jesus decided to show them that the story of crucifixion and resurrection was exactly what they should expect—and that it was the reason all the other stories were there at all. It worked. "Did not our hearts burn within us while he talked to us on the road, while he opened to us the Scriptures?" (Lk. 24:32).

The story beneath the story is just about the most powerful one there is, and not just for worship, but for mission. A Jewish or a Muslim friend might well misunderstand your attempts to explain the divinity of Jesus or the resurrection. But going back to Abraham and explaining how the whole thing points to the cross, like Jesus does here, might just do the trick.

ii

GOD'S MISSION

Then he opened their minds to
understand the Scriptures, and said
to them, "Thus it is written, that
the Christ should suffer and on the
third day rise from the dead, and that
repentance and forgiveness of sins
should be proclaimed in his name to all
nations, beginning from Jerusalem."
(Luke 24:45-47)

God has a mission.[1] It's the biggest mission there is: to fill
the earth with his glory by covering it with people who bear
his image. It's the oldest mission in existence, dating from
humanity's birth. It's also a dangerous mission, for which
many thousands of people die every year, and many more
are beaten, tortured, imprisoned or dispossessed. In Luke
24, just after his resurrection, Jesus does a Bible study with

---

1   I am thankful to David Devenish for much of what follows.

his disciples to show them that God's massive, ancient and perilous mission lies at the heart of the Old Testament story. The mission is this: "that repentance and forgiveness of sins should be proclaimed in his name to all nations, beginning from Jerusalem."

It might not have looked like that to start with. Even the biggest avalanche begins with a small shudder. But that's the mission, and like all good missions, it starts with a problem to be solved. In the first few chapters of Genesis, we encounter the problem of sin and the need for repentance, the reality of judgment, and then in chapter 10 we are introduced to the nations of the world, all seventy of them (remember that number). Seventy sinful nations all in need of forgiveness. That's Act One.

Act Two takes a leap across to Ur, in modern day Iraq, where a completely unremarkable man called Abram is given a completely remarkable promise. "In you," Yahweh says to this pagan from an idol-worshiping city, "all the families of the earth shall be blessed." Fast forward a bit, and Abraham's wayward grandson Jacob gets his name changed to Israel and then has twelve sons (remember that number), who form the heads of the twelve tribes of Israel. God's plan to bless the earth is well underway.

In the next few centuries, Israel gets both a land and a king but doesn't really take its call to be a blessing that seriously, and the nation ends up splitting into two chunks, north (Israel) and south (Judah). As we move into Act Three, where the prophets are the main characters, we find that Israel only sends one—one!—missionary to the nations, and even he is so unhappy about it, he ends up doing time inside a fish to teach him a lesson. Even so, the prophets start getting glimpses of God's promise to bless and teach other nations through them:

> It is too light a thing that you should be my servant to raise up the tribes of Jacob and to bring back the preserved of Israel; I will make you as a light for the nations, that my salvation may reach to the end of the earth. (Isaiah 49:6)

When the Old Testament concludes, this still hasn't happened. But the mission of God to bless all the families on earth remains, hovering in the background.

Cue the lights for Act Four: "The book of the genealogy of Jesus Christ, the son of David, the son of Abraham" (Mt. 1:1). With the birth of Jesus, suddenly everything changes. An old saint gives thanks that "a light for revelation to the Gentiles" has been born (Lk. 2:32). Jesus gathers and sends a group of twelve men, representing Israel, and then a group of seventy, representing the nations of the world (remember those numbers?). He then sends out his followers as missionaries to the ends of the earth, to proclaim repentance and forgiveness of sins in all nations. Start in Jerusalem, he says, but soon you'll be in Judea, Samaria, and even the furthest corners of the world.

And so, in Act Five, the mission of God goes flying out of the blocks. Thousands repent in Jerusalem, Philip preaches in Samaria, Peter sees the Spirit fall on Gentiles, and Paul's team won't stop moving until all the nations have been blessed:

> Jesus Christ our Lord, through whom we have received grace and apostleship to bring about the obedience of

faith for the sake of his name among *all the nations*. (Romans 1:4-5, my italics)

For I tell you that Christ became a servant to the circumcised to show God's truthfulness, in order to confirm the promises given to the patriarchs, and *in order that the Gentiles might glorify God* for his mercy ... and thus I make it my ambition to preach the gospel, *not where Christ has already been named*. (Romans 15:8-9, 20, my italics)

These people were on fire. They got kicked out of homes and towns, took heavy beatings, were stoned, got shipwrecked and often got killed. So have millions of God's people since then. Why? Because they have grasped that God's mission was never for his people just to hang out together, or even just to study the Bible and pray together. It was "that repentance and forgiveness of sins should be proclaimed in all nations." That's what drove Abraham, Moses, Isaiah, Jesus, Paul, Phoebe, St Patrick, John Calvin, William Carey, Hudson Taylor and Amy Carmichael. It drives every nameless hero who loses career, family, home or even life to accomplish God's mission. Jim Elliot was right: "He is no fool who gives what he cannot keep to gain what he cannot lose."[2]

The mission of God will prevail, because Yahweh made a promise to Abraham to bless all the families of the earth, and he's going to keep it. There's still a long way to go, because

---

2 From the diary of Jim Elliot, 28 October 1949. Elliot, a missionary to the Auca Indians in Ecuador, was hacked to death with wooden machetes for preaching the gospel on 8 January 1956.

the best estimates suggest that there are still at least five thousand people groups who have never heard the gospel. But God's mission is advancing. In Nepal in 1960, there were twenty believers; there are now a quarter of a million. In Kyrgyzstan in 1986, there was one believer; now there's four thousand. In AD 30, one hundred and twenty people on earth named Jesus as Lord; now there's about a billion. God's mission is old, and huge, and dangerous. It's going to succeed.

And unlike some gospel stories, it's waiting to be completed. Who's in?

MOUNT MORIAH

[God] said, "Take your son, your only
son Isaac, whom you love, and go to the
land of Moriah, and offer him there
as a burnt offering on one of the
mountains of which I shall tell you."
(Genesis 22:2)

It is the middle of the night when a 110-year-old man hears the voice of God. Abraham has heard this voice before. Years before, the voice told him to leave his land and start travelling with no map and no destination, so he did. The voice promised him billions of descendants; he believed. It told him to circumcise both himself and all the males in his household, so he did. The voice asked him to trust that his ninety-year-old wife would have a baby. He did, and Sarah nursed a child. But now, as he hears the familiar voice again, Abraham sinks back on to his bed, shocked eyes staring into the darkness. There will be no more sleep for Abraham this night.

But Abraham's track record of hearing and obeying the voice has set him in good stead, and he trusts the God who has asked him to sacrifice the son he loves. Early in the morning, he wakes his son, takes a couple of servants, and heads off for a three-day hike to Mount Moriah. The lack of an animal to sacrifice makes Isaac curious, but Abraham only reminds him of God's provision. However, as he ties his son down to the altar, the doubts surely must have flooded his mind: *What about God's promise to bless the world through my children? How can this be Yahweh's will? Did I simply imagine he was telling me to do this?* Yet in disciplined faith, learned from a lifetime of trusting obedience, Abraham raises the knife and prepares to plunge it into the love of his life and the hope of the nations. It is then, and only then, that God tells Abraham not to harm the boy and provides a replacement sacrifice for him.

Frequently, we stop the story there, celebrating the faithfulness of God and his revelation as Yahweh-will-provide, reflecting on the substitute ram, marveling at Abraham's faith, and rightly seeing in him an example for our own lives. But let's read on to the end of the story:

> And the angel of the LORD called to Abraham a second time from heaven and said, "By myself I have sworn, declares the LORD, because you have done this and have not withheld your son, your only son, I will surely bless you, and I will surely multiply your offspring as the stars of heaven and as the sand that is on the seashore."
>
> (Genesis 22:15-17)

Yahweh, with his eyes fixed on the altar, is able to tell Abraham: Now I know, for certain, that you love me, because you did not spare your own son. I knew you loved me before, but now your faithfulness has been demonstrated once and for all, so I promise I will bless you throughout all generations.

Four millennia later, as disciples of Jesus, with our eyes fixed on the cross, we can see an offering that shows an even greater love, as the true hope of the nations died for all people. We are able to tell God the Father: Now I know, for certain, that you love me, because you did not spare your own Son. I knew you loved me before, but now your faithfulness has been demonstrated once and for all, so I promise I will bless your name throughout all generations.

The events in Genesis 22 were always designed by God to direct us to the cross, right down to the geographical details. A thousand years after Abraham wiped the ram's blood from his knife, a prophet called Gad approaches King David and tells him to build a second altar there, in the same place as Abraham's, and to seek Yahweh's forgiveness for the people (2 Sam. 24:18). Solomon, David's son, later builds the temple of Yahweh on this very site in Jerusalem: the place where God meets humanity, sacrifice is offered, and forgiveness for the people is found (2 Chr. 3:1).

And about a thousand years after that, a third altar is established on Mount Moriah, about half a mile from the temple, at a place known locally as the hill of the skull. It is like other altars in many ways—made of wood, a place where God meets humanity, sacrifice is offered, and forgiveness for the people is found—but in one respect Moriah's third altar looks totally different from the previous two, and

from every other altar ever constructed. This altar is shaped
like a cross.

iv
—

THE SEED

Now the promises were spoken to Abraham
and to his seed. He does not say, "And to
seeds," as referring to many, but rather to
one, "And to your seed," that is, Christ.
(Galatians 3:16, NASB)

I'm often amazed at the difference one letter can make. On
January 2, 2007, CNN issued a formal apology to a presiden-
tial candidate because of one letter, as footage of a terrorist
manhunt was accompanied with the caption "Where is
Obama?" Similarly, you can imagine the fall-out from a card
saying "Wish you were her."

One letter was never more important than in God's
promises to Abraham, though.[1] Paul is adamant about this in

---

1 Some will object that although there is only one letter's difference
between the singular and plural in English, there are more than that
in both Greek and Hebrew. But the point stands about crucial differences in meaning turning on slight differences in spelling.

Galatians 3: the fact that God made the promises to Abraham's "seed," rather than his "seeds," suggests that ultimately one person, rather than a group of people, would fulfill them. The promises to Abraham—which pretty much the whole Bible is about—are not going to be fulfilled in a random group of descendants, or even in God's chosen nation of Israel, but in one person: Christ.

So what were the promises to Abraham? For that, we need to go back to Genesis:

> Yahweh appeared to Abram and said, "I will give this land to your seed." (Genesis 12:7, WEB footnote)

> I will greatly multiply your seed as the stars of the heavens and as the sand which is on the seashore; and your seed shall possess the gate of their enemies. In your seed all the nations of the earth shall be blessed, because you have obeyed My voice. (Genesis 22:17-18, NASB)

I count four promises: 1) The seed will be given the land of Israel; 2) The seed will be incredibly numerous; 3) The seed will have jurisdiction over his enemies; and 4) The seed will be a blessing to all the nations of the earth. Quite a sweeping set of promises!

Many people believe the promises belong to the whole of ethnic Israel but one crucial letter clears up the mistake—the promises are for the "seed," not "seeds." It sounds strange that the "seed," Christ, and not Israel as a whole, would inherit the land of Israel forever and be incredibly numerous, blessing nations and subduing enemies. Yet that's what Paul says.

In fact, God's plan had always been to focus his promise on one person. Even in Genesis 22, the "seed" cannot mean all of Abraham's descendants, because the promise runs through Isaac and not Ishmael. The next generation, the promise narrows again, to Jacob and not Esau. And so it goes on, getting more specific each time: Judah ahead of his brothers, then the line of Jesse, then David, then Solomon, and finally Christ. God has always wanted to focus all his power and promises through one person.

It was Jesus (the "seed"), and not ethnic Israel (the "seeds"), who would inherit the land of Israel forever, be as numerous as the stars, rule over his enemies and bless the entire world. This, of course, raises the questions: in what sense has Jesus been given the land, and in what sense is he "numerous"? For the answer, we need to return to Galatians:

> For you are all sons of God through faith in Christ Jesus. *For as many of you as were baptized into Christ have put on Christ.* There is neither Jew nor Greek, there is neither slave nor free, there is neither male nor female; for you are all one in Christ Jesus. *And if you are Christ's, then you are Abraham's seed, and heirs according to the promise.*
> (Galatians 3:26-29, NKJV, my italics)

Can you see what Paul is saying? Everyone baptized into Christ has "put on" Christ, and somehow been incorporated into him. That means that Abraham's seed, Christ, includes everyone who has been baptized into him. If I put a piece of chewing gum in my mouth and climb Table Mountain, the chewing gum gets to the summit too because it is inside of me, and it is the same with us when we are in Christ. So the land, and in fact the whole earth (Rom. 4:13), are inherited by those who have "put on" Abraham's seed, Christ. And the blessing to all nations comes through those who are in Christ: you, me, the Apostle Paul, William Wilberforce, Gladys Aylward, Desmond Tutu.

It's not an easy idea, so let's use an analogy. Imagine that in 1840, God promises a Scot named Hugh Fleming that his seed will save millions of lives around the world. But when Hugh dies, none of his eight children have saved anybody. In 1928, however, his son Alexander discovers Penicillin, marking the start of modern antibiotics and eventually saving millions of lives. God's promise is true.

Now imagine that the rest of Hugh's surviving children reject Alexander and Penicillin. That wouldn't undermine God's promise, would it? No! But if they wanted to inherit the promise and save millions of lives they'd have to join their brother, tell everyone about Penicillin and distribute it as far as possible. But—and here's the twist—that option is not only open to Hugh's children, but to anybody else who shows confidence in Alexander's discovery. The true heirs of the promise to Hugh are not the natural children. The true heirs of the promise are the thousands of doctors and researchers around the world who have faith in Penicillin, and do all they can to spread it throughout the world to save people. "If you are Christ's, you are Abraham's seed, and heirs according to the promise."

You and I, along with the rest of God's global church, are the heirs of the earth. We're the hope of the world. Because of one letter.

V

THE PASSOVER

For I will pass through the land of
Egypt that night, and I will strike
all the firstborn in the land of
Egypt, both man and beast; and on
all the gods of Egypt I will execute
judgments: I am the LORD. The blood
shall be a sign for you, on the houses
where you are. And when I see the
blood, I will pass over you, and no
plague will befall you to destroy
you, when I strike the land of Egypt.
(Exodus 12:12-13)

My father-in-law drives like a maniac. He tears around town in
his red truck, speeding, going the wrong way down one-way
streets, running red lights, cutting off other drivers, and even
going around roundabouts anticlockwise. Yet in twenty years
of driving his red truck, he has never once been stopped or

cautioned by the police. His red truck is a fire engine, with a flashing blue light on top. And the flashing blue light makes all the difference.

We are all familiar with symbols of membership that allow us certain privileges, whether or not people have any idea who we are. I get into Britain because of my passport, not my knowledge of the rules of cricket. ATMs give me cash because I can enter my PIN, not because of my ability to handle money. What matters is not my behavior on the day in question, or even my moral character as a whole; what matters is the number, the thumbprint, the document, or the flashing blue light. It makes all the difference.

Perhaps the most powerful example of this in history was the Passover. Pharaoh remains adamant: the Israelites will not go free, despite having his nation carpet-bombed with frogs, gnats, boils, locusts and the rest. Moses threatens that the firstborn of every Egyptian family will be killed unless he releases the slaves. Pharaoh says no. So Yahweh sends the destroying angel through Egypt at night, killing every firstborn son, bringing catastrophic destruction and grief upon the nation. Only the Israelites are exempt, protected from this plague by an extraordinary symbol of the grace of God:

> Go and select lambs for yourselves according to your clans, and kill the Passover lamb. Take a bunch of hyssop and dip it in the blood that is in the basin, and touch the lintel and the two doorposts with the blood that is in the basin … For the LORD will pass through to strike the Egyptians, and when he sees the blood on the lintel and on the two doorposts, the LORD will pass over the door

> and will not allow the destroyer to enter your houses to
> strike you. (Exodus 12:21-23)

The only thing separating the Israelites from death was the
blood on their doorposts. Good behavior didn't shelter them
from destruction, nor ongoing obedience to God, nor an elaborate deal by which they promised to follow him forever. The
blood on the doorpost made all the difference.

Just think for a moment about the scandal of this arrangement. In some cases, the Egyptians facing Yahweh's judgment
may have been better people than some of the Israelites who
were saved. The wicked Israelites received the same privileges
as the godly ones, simply because blood decorated their
doorpost. That red smear wasn't one of the factors God took
into consideration when deciding who to rescue and who to
destroy. It was the only factor. Like the flashing blue light on
the fire engine, the blood on the doorpost was the symbol of
membership, and it made (quite literally) all the difference.

That is grace. Grace is how God works. When we look
at Jesus, our sacrificial Passover lamb (1 Cor. 5:7), we see the
same principle in operation. We see that our rescue from
the slavery of sin rests not on our performance, but on his
sacrifice. We see that through faith in his blood, rather than
through our efforts, we are not destroyed. We see that when
the Father looks at our lives, he justifies us on the basis of Jesus'
obedience and law-keeping and zeal for God, not on ours. The
only factor, the *only* factor, that he takes into consideration is
whether or not we have cried out for the blood of the Lamb
to save us.

It makes all the difference.

THE CURTAIN

And Jesus cried out again with a loud
voice and yielded up his spirit. And
behold, the curtain of the temple was
torn in two, from top to bottom. And the
earth shook, and the rocks were split.
(Matthew 27:50-51)

A curtain separated heaven and earth. It might not sound like much, but from Sinai to Calvary an embroidered sheet of twisted linen divided sinful people from their holy God. Every Israelite knew that Yahweh lived in their midst, but for fifteen centuries, all they could see was a curtain, up to sixty feet high and three inches thick.

The curtain kept the people apart from the awe-inspiring and dangerous Holy One on the other side, and reminded them that they were not up to the standard required to approach him. Occasionally in Israel's history, individuals forgot this, and tried to approach Yahweh as if no curtain existed: out of defiance (Lev. 10:1-2), out of curiosity (1 Sam. 6:19-20), or even out of a misguided desire to help (2 Sam. 6:6-7). The instant death that met each one, while tragic for the individuals concerned, served as a warning to the rest of the people: God is profoundly holy, and you are not.

It first appeared around 1445 BC, when God gave Moses instructions on how to build the tabernacle. This huge tent had a courtyard about the size of an Olympic swimming pool, in which priests offered animal sacrifices. At the back was a smaller structure called the tent of meeting, divided from the courtyard by a linen curtain, woven in blue, purple and scarlet. Only priests could enter here. Beyond this hung a second curtain, sometimes called a "veil," which marked off the Holy of Holies. Only one man could go through this curtain, only once a year, and when he did, he attached golden bells to his robe and a rope to his ankle so people would know if he had died before the presence of Yahweh. So actually, two curtains divided the people from Yahweh (although the New Testament often talks about them as one), offering the people a powerful picture of how unapproachable Yahweh was. One curtain, separating the people from the priests. Another curtain, separating the priests from their God. Sixty feet high and three inches thick.

Think for a moment about the different security areas that you have in a bank. In the public spaces, open to everyone, there is very little real money. You know the money is in the bank somewhere, and you make transactions accordingly, but almost all of it remains behind coded doors. Like the Israelites in the courtyard of the tabernacle, you cannot actually see the very thing you came for; you rely on others, authorized to act on your behalf, to access it for you. Only the bank staff, though, like the priests in Israel, are allowed through the coded doors into the secure areas.

But even the bank employees don't have access to the vault. Somewhere, deep inside the building, is a depository, where millions are stored. It is maximum security, with a giant steel gate that can only be opened with a fingerprint and a retinal scan; perhaps only the manager has access, and even he hardly ever goes inside. It is awkward for the manager, inaccessible for the bank staff, and utterly impossible to get near for the likes of you and me. Even the first locked door is six feet high and three inches thick.

Now imagine you walk into your local bank, and all the coded doors are lying in pieces on the floor. As you peer through into the mysterious world on the other side, you can see an equally shattered steel gate, and behind it, all the money you could ever have imagined in nice neat piles. You wonder what you should do, until the manager approaches you, tells you about the new bank policy, and cheerfully invites you to go into the vault and help yourself to all the money you want.

Now change the picture: you are a temple attendant in AD 30. A beautifully embroidered curtain has isolated you from the presence of Yahweh for fifteen hundred years. Yet because of the death of Jesus of Nazareth, the barrier that prevented you approaching God has been destroyed forever, irrevocably torn from top to bottom. The Messiah's death was so definitive, his sacrifice so sufficient, that the very laws of physics could not hold together this mighty symbol of God's unapproachability. It lies ripped in half on the floor in front of you. All sixty feet of it.

The curtain is torn. The animal sacrifices and bells and security codes and retinal scans are no longer needed; the vault of God's presence is open, and the Manager beckons us inside. So, as Hebrews 10:19-22 invites us, "since we have confidence to enter the holy places by the blood of Jesus, by the new and living way that he opened for us through the curtain … let us draw near with a true heart in full assurance of faith."

VII

THE DAY OF ATONEMENT

Then Aaron shall cast lots for the
two goats: one lot for the LORD and
the other lot for the scapegoat. And
Aaron shall bring the goat on which the
LORD's lot fell, and offer it as a sin
offering. But the goat on which the
lot fell to be the scapegoat shall be
presented alive before the LORD, to make
atonement upon it, and to let it go as
the scapegoat into the wilderness.
(Leviticus 16:8-10, NKJV)

What do the following phrases all have in common? A drop
in the bucket; at their wits' end; bite the dust; by the skin of
my teeth; give up the ghost; sour grapes; the powers that be;
rise and shine. The answer: they all originate from the Bible
but no longer have religious meanings, because they have
entered everyday English. Maybe the best example of this, and

certainly the most important in the biblical story, is the word "scapegoat" from Leviticus 16.

The image of the scapegoat goes back three and a half thousand years, to the Day of Atonement. On this pivotal day in the Jewish calendar, still celebrated by Jews as *Yom Kippur*, the high priest entered the Most Holy Place to make atonement for the sins of the people. On no other day in the year was he allowed to do this. Because of the holiness of God, if he did, he would die. On the Day of Atonement, though, he would take two goats. One of them would be sacrificed and its blood smeared around the altar and the Holy Place, like a normal sin offering. The other was the scapegoat, and it would be sent out into the wilderness carrying the sins of the people, never to be seen again. It took the blame that rightly belonged to others, an idea we still associate with a "scapegoat" in secular English today.

It is important to understand that these two goats represented the two aspects of Yahweh's forgiveness: cleansing and separation. The first goat was all about cleansing from sin, and was primarily Godward—it dealt with the uncleanness of sin, and restored Israel to right relationship with Yahweh. Sin leads to death, which brings guilt, so our guilt is cleansed by the death of an innocent.

The scapegoat, on the other hand, demonstrated separation from sin, and was primarily manward—it showed Israel that their sins had been taken away from them as far as the east is from the west, and that they would never see them again. Sin leads to shame; our shame is removed by the exile of an innocent. It's all very well having someone forgive you for theft, murder or adultery, but if the result of your sin (a pile of stolen money, a corpse, a jilted husband) is sitting at the end of your bed when you wake up every day, it's far harder to accept it. For Israel's sake, and ours, both cleansing and separation are needed when God forgives, so that not just guilt but also shame is overcome.

When the priest put his hands on the goat, laid Israel's sins upon it and sent it into the desert, Israel knew that their transgressions had not only been forgiven, but forgotten; not just washed away from God's sight, but taken away from ours. Picture it: as the priest led the goat out of the camp and into the wilderness, the people would be able to see all their jealousy and greed and lust and pride taken away with it, and banished from their presence forever. One innocent animal effectively *became sin* for the people, and left the camp to signify the complete removal of all shame.

Wonderfully, like so much else in Leviticus, both goats pointed forward to an even more dramatic picture of forgiveness:

> For our sake he *made him to be sin* who knew no sin, so that in him we might become the righteousness of God.
> (2 Corinthians 5:21, my italics)

Now, I guess we're all familiar with Jesus as the first goat, the sin offering that cleanses us before God. We sinned, he didn't, he got killed, we don't. It's true, it's glorious, and it's widely thought about, taught about and sung about. But what we may not consider so often is that Jesus is also our scapegoat: he took our sin upon himself and left the camp, separating us from our sins, and removing the shame that separated us from

God. Golgotha wasn't a suburb of Jerusalem, but an execution
site outside the city walls. This may not seem significant to us,
but to a Jewish person who understood Leviticus, it could not
be more important:

> For the bodies of those animals whose blood is brought
> into the holy places by the high priest as a sacrifice for
> sin are burned outside the camp. So Jesus also suffered
> outside the gate in order to sanctify the people through
> his own blood. Therefore let us go to him outside the
> camp and bear the reproach he endured. (Hebrews
> 13:11-13)

Jesus died outside the city walls, outside the camp, to demonstrate that he was the way in which our sin wasn't just cleansed,
but removed from us. As he walked out of the city founded by
his power and his by rights, carrying a cross upon his bleeding
back, he carried the shame of everything you and I have ever
done. He carried it out of the camp, into the wilderness, onto
the cross, never to be seen again. The ultimate scapegoat.

The Day of Atonement was pretty amazing, really. It was a
day of celebration and sins forgiven. It was the day on which
God said the people should proclaim the year of Jubilee
(every fifty years), the year of property redistribution showing
the past was dealt with and everyone could start again. It
demonstrated that those terrible consequences of sin, guilt
and shame were overcome. It showed that the effects of sin
on both people and God had been atoned for, forgiven to the
uttermost. And it pointed forwards, in a spectacularly visual
way, to another Day of Atonement, and the astonishing reality

that at the cross of Jesus, death would be killed and separation would be removed completely:

> God presented him as a sacrifice of atonement, through the shedding of his blood. (Romans 3:25, NIV)

THE ARK OF THE COVENANT

> They sent therefore and gathered
> together all the lords of the
> Philistines and said, "Send away the
> ark of the God of Israel, and let it
> return to its own place, that it may
> not kill us and our people."
> (1 Samuel 5:11)

For a thousand years, God lived in a box. Theologians, don't freak out: I know God fills heaven and earth, and no box can contain him. But again and again in Scripture, a small box is described as housing the presence of Yahweh. Made of acacia wood, and measuring four feet long, two feet wide and two feet high, it contained two stones with laws written on them, an urn with manna, and a staff which had sprouted flowers. It all sounds a bit peculiar to us, but that's where the power and presence of Yahweh could be found for around a millennium. It was called the ark of the covenant.

The journey of this box is one of my favorite gospel stories, because it displays both the utter grace and the utter holiness of Yahweh. It shows his grace, because it indicates his desire to live amongst his people, even when they were stupid and sinful. He could have chosen to remain up a fearsomely high and dangerous mountain, far removed from sinful humanity. That's what I would have done. But instead, he decided to dwell in something portable, so that he could live among the people of God wherever they went. That's as unexpected as the CEO of Procter and Gamble choosing an office on the factory floor in Huddersfield, or the Ambassador to India living in a Mumbai slum. The ark is a box of grace.

But it is also a box of holiness. When it is first constructed in the fifteenth century BC, Yahweh gives detailed instructions on how to build it, how to carry it and how to approach it, because if anyone approaches the holiness of God without due care, they will die. Quickly, the Israelites discover that Yahweh's intense holiness means the box has tremendous power. When the priests carrying the ark reach the banks of the River Jordan, the river stops flowing, just like that. When they step out the other side, the river comes crashing back again and overflows its banks. When the ark is carried around Jericho, one of the ancient world's great fortified cities, the walls come crashing down. The ark of the covenant could save lives as well as destroy them, stop rivers as well as flood them, rescue Israel as well as trounce her enemies. It was quite a box.

This immense power, though, made the ark of the covenant something of a talisman for Israel. They began to believe that the ark would save them independently of their obedience, and started seeing the box as the source of power, rather than the God who dwelt within. When you consider the holiness of Yahweh, it is no surprise that this "lucky charm" approach backfired spectacularly:

> "Let us bring the ark of the covenant of the LORD here from Shiloh, that it may come among us and save us from the power of our enemies." ... So the Philistines fought, and Israel was defeated, and they fled, every man to his home ... And the ark of God was captured. (1 Samuel 4:3, 10-11)

The ark of Yahweh was taken by the Philistines around 1100 BC. They knew Israel's God lived in the box, so they believed Yahweh would now be fighting on their side. But a little knowledge is a dangerous thing, and they decided to put the ark in the temple of their god, Dagon. The Philistines didn't realize that the real God, the God of Abraham, Isaac and Jacob, in all his unapproachable holiness, inhabited the box. The result is predictable, and almost comic:

> ... behold, Dagon had fallen face downward on the ground before the ark of the LORD. So they took Dagon and put him back in his place. But when they rose early on the next morning, behold, Dagon had fallen face downward on the ground before the ark of the LORD, and the head of Dagon and both his hands were lying cut off on the threshold. Only the trunk of Dagon was left to him. This is why the priests of Dagon and all who enter the house of Dagon do not tread on the threshold of Dagon in Ashdod to this day. (1 Samuel 5:3-5)

I'm not surprised. I wouldn't tread there either. But it gets worse, because the entire town starts getting afflicted with tumors because of the ark. The Philistines respond with blind panic, and send it on to the town next door, where the same thing happens, and then again in the town after that. Finally they get the message: that Yahweh is in the box, and he is not to be messed with—and they send the ark back to Israel.

Even in Israel, the holiness of Yahweh and the box he lives in cause chaos. The first Israelites to see it make the mistake of peering inside, and seventy men in that village are killed. Terrified, they put the ark in the house of a man called Abinadab, where it remains for twenty years lest it kill anyone else. David, recently anointed king, then comes to bring the ark up to Jerusalem, and gets Abinadab's sons to drive the cart carrying it—but one of them, Uzzah, reaches out and touches the ark when the oxen stumble, and he immediately dies as well. The ark may not be in a tabernacle at this point, but the God who lives within is the same as he always has been. There is no room for a careless or flippant approach to the holiness of Yahweh—as Uzzah, son of Abinadab, would most surely have known.

After all that, and with much celebration, the ark arrives in Jerusalem in about 1010 BC, and is eventually housed in Solomon's newly built temple in around 950, with more sacrifices than could be counted. The box had lost none of its splendor over the past five centuries: when placed in the temple, the glory cloud of Yahweh descends with such intensity that the priests are completely overwhelmed and left incapable of doing their jobs. And in the temple the ark remains, the focal point of Jewish worship and the centerpiece of Jewish hope.

That's not quite the end of the story, though. When the Babylonians invade and drag Judah into exile, the ark gets destroyed, which looks like a total disaster. But the prophet Ezekiel, to his astonishment, sees the presence of Yahweh actually leaving the temple and coming to live among the Jewish people, with God revealing his name as Yahweh-is-there. Jeremiah goes further, and prophesies that the ark will not be rebuilt, or even pined for, in the age to come. So, though many speculate about it and Indiana Jones thought he found it, the ark of the covenant is not on earth any longer. Instead, it is exactly where you would expect it to be:

> Then God's temple in heaven was opened, and the ark of his covenant was seen within his temple. There were flashes of lightning, rumblings, peals of thunder, an earthquake, and heavy hail. (Revelation 11:19)

Presence and distance, grace and holiness. That's the ark. That's our God.

THE TEMPLE

> When all the people of Israel saw the
> fire come down and the glory of the
> LORD on the temple, they bowed down
> with their faces to the ground on the
> pavement and worshiped and gave thanks
> to the LORD, saying, "For he is good, for
> his steadfast love endures forever."
> (2 Chronicles 7:3)

In the beginning God created a temple.[1]

That might sound like nonsense. Solomon's temple wasn't built until the eleventh century BC, and the world was created long before that. But if you look carefully through Scripture, you'll find that God's Word begins and ends with temples. You'll notice that temple imagery in the Bible is more about the presence of God than about any particular building, and

---

1 This chapter is based on the fascinating study of G. K. Beale, *The Temple and the Church's Mission* (Leicester: IVP, 2004).

that temple language tells a very clear gospel story about the presence of God filling the earth. After all, as Paul remarked in Acts 17:24, the God who made heaven and earth and everything else doesn't live in temples built by hands.

The Garden of Eden was the original temple. It was the place where God lived, and a place of such holiness that sin could not remain within it. Like every temple, the garden had a priest, a man appointed to serve it and keep it—the exact same responsibilities Israel's priests would be given later in the story. Like both the tabernacle and later the temple in Jerusalem, the holy presence of God in the garden was guarded by cherubim. The garden was covered in fruit of course, and a tree grew at the very center. Decorative fruit adorned the tabernacle and the temple too, and a golden lampstand shaped like a tree stood in the center. Like the two main temple visions in Scripture, a river flowed through the middle of the Garden of Eden, and its entrance faced east. I don't think all that can be coincidence.

Temples begin the story. They end it too. Read the vision of the new heavens and the new earth in Revelation 21-22, and you'll find that the whole of creation has become a temple. John sees the new creation as a giant cubic structure—the same shape as the Most Holy Place—where, temple-like, nothing unclean ever enters. The whole vision reminds us of the temple Ezekiel saw, right down to the detail of the river:

> And on the banks, on both sides of the river, there will grow all kinds of trees for food ... they will bear fresh fruit every month, because the water for them flows from the sanctuary. Their fruit will be for food, and their leaves for healing. (Ezekiel 47:12)

> Also, on either side of the river, the tree of life with its
> twelve kinds of fruit, yielding its fruit each month. The
> leaves of the tree were for the healing of the nations.
> (Revelation 22:2)

Pretty similar, aren't they? Yet one big difference stands out: in
Revelation, the city has no temple. That's the point! Instead,
God's glory fills the whole of creation. In other words, *the
entire new creation has become a temple*, a place where God lives
in uninterrupted and untainted glory.

The Bible starts with the Garden of Eden as a temple, with
God in the middle, and ends with the whole earth as a temple,
with God everywhere. The question is: So what?

The temple was all about God's presence. When God
instructed Moses to build a tabernacle, he told him to build
it in three parts to illustrate this. There was the Most Holy
Place (or the Holy of Holies), where God lived; the Holy Place
(or the tent of meeting), where only priests could go; and the
surrounding court, where normal Israelites could come. Later,
the temple had the same structure, with three different layers
of holiness, if you like. On one hand, Israel benefited greatly
from having the presence of Yahweh in their midst, since the
temple was where heaven met earth. That's why the scene in
2 Chronicles 7 is so dramatic; the presence of Yahweh filled
the entire temple in glory and fire. On the other hand, the
Jews were protected from Yahweh's holiness by being kept
separate, through this three-part system.

But this separation was never the ultimate plan. Remember,
God intended his presence to fill the whole earth, so the
Jerusalem temple was only an interim measure. One day, the

presence of God would break out of the Most Holy Place and start filling the entire cosmos, as had been the idea ever since Eden. With the cross of Jesus, this became possible. The ripping of the temple curtain not only brought the world into God's presence, it also took God's presence into the world. Through Jesus, God's temple suddenly started spreading rapidly, spreading over the whole of creation.

That's where you and I come in:

> Do you not know that you are God's temple and that God's Spirit dwells in you? If anyone destroys God's temple, God will destroy him. For God's temple is holy, and you are that temple. (1 Corinthians 3:16-17)

> For we are the temple of the living God; as God said, "I will make my dwelling among them and walk among them, and I will be their God, and they shall be my people." (2 Corinthians 6:16)

> You are ... built on the foundation of the apostles and prophets, Christ Jesus himself being the cornerstone, in whom the whole structure, being joined together, grows into a holy temple in the Lord. (Ephesians 2:19-21)

God's Spirit, the glory and the fire, fills the earth through us. The presence of God was concentrated in a garden, then a tent, then a temple, but now it is in the church of God. When Acts begins, the Most Holy Place measures the size of an upper room; by the time Acts finishes, God's presence has reached Rome; today, it stretches from Antarctica to Alaska. But the day draws ever nearer when his glory will fill the whole of creation, in one giant temple from Bethlehem to Betelgeuse:

> The city has no need of sun or moon to shine on it, for the glory of God gives it light, and its lamp is the Lamb. By its light will the nations walk, and the kings of the earth will bring their glory into it. (Revelation 21:23-24)

I can't wait.

ACT THREE

POETS AND PROPHETS

SUFFERING'S ANSWER

Then Job arose and tore his robe and
shaved his head and fell on the ground
and worshiped. And he said, "Naked I
came from my mother's womb, and naked
shall I return. The LORD gave, and the
LORD has taken away; blessed be the
name of the LORD."
(Job 1:20-21)

If you've experienced suffering, you've got to love Job. I doubt anything ever written has been as brutally honest about the problem of pain. All the difficult questions are raised, and all the easy answers are dismissed. All in all, it's one of the most profound, moving and challenging of stories there is.

A good man experiences massive and inexplicable suffering. Lightning destroys his possessions and raiders take his livestock, a hurricane kills his children and his servants are struck down by enemies, and then painful sores break out, covering his body from head to toe. We then spend the rest of the poem exploring the various answers that can be given to the simple question: why does suffering happen?

Firstly, let's look at some of the wrong answers Job is presented with. Lots of the easy explanations people give are torpedoed by the book of Job, of which we can only mention four:

1. *Suffering isn't real—it's just an illusion*. Job does not go near such an answer, and the writer pulls no punches in saying both how real and how unpleasant human suffering can often be. Making light of bereavement or cancer doesn't make them go away.

2. *God doesn't cause suffering, Satan does*. Although often repeated, and seemingly helpful, believing this comes at a massive cost, because it implies that God is not really in control—he's officially in power, like King Richard in *Robin Hood*, but unable to stop the Sheriff of Nottingham running riot. A friend of mine had a series of problems buying a house recently, and told me that whenever things went right, people said "Praise God!" but when they went wrong, they told him it was opposition from the devil. This is not always true. And it certainly wasn't for Job: Yahweh gave, and Yahweh has taken away; blessed be the name of Yahweh.

3. *God is not good*. This is the response of Job's wife, who urges Job to curse God and die. Job will not have any of it: "Shall we receive good from God, and shall we not receive evil?"

(2:10). God's goodness is not on the table. There must be another reason.

4. *We get what we deserve, so if you're suffering, it's your fault.* This, to oversimplify, is where Job's three friends are coming from; they start down this line of reasoning early on, and get more and more strident about it as the poem continues. But this, apart from being a very unpleasant thing to say to someone in pain, is also wrong, because good people like Job sometimes suffer and wicked people sometimes prosper (21:7). People who preach a gospel of health, wealth and prosperity for all God's children have simply not reckoned with Job, let alone Jesus.

However, though the book of Job raises and dismisses a number of bad responses to suffering, it also gives several good ones which we would do well to learn from:

1. *Silence.* Job's friends begin with silence, and it is absolutely appropriate. When someone grieves their family, possessions and health, a cheerful "it'll all be okay" is useless. Sitting with them, sharing their grief and waiting in silence is far better.

2. *God is still in charge, and God is still good, even though his idea of goodness might not always be the same as mine.* Despite Job's terrible pain and confusion, both he and his friends hold fast to these truths. In contrast, if I am honest, I can sometimes make God smaller to account for things I don't understand. We mustn't purchase our answers at the expense of either God's goodness or his sovereignty.

3. *Resurrection is coming.* About half way through the book, Job hits on this extraordinary piece of revelation, and while it doesn't make suffering go away, it certainly helps put it in perspective. When Job starts out, he believes that death is the end, the grave is a one-way street, and therefore suffering in this life will have the last word. When resurrection is factored in, though, hope of a better future awakens: "I know that my Redeemer lives, and at the last he will stand upon the earth. And after my skin has been thus destroyed, yet in my flesh I shall see God" (19:25-26).

4. *Yahweh is far, far greater than we are, and has purposes in the world we know nothing about.* This, ultimately, is the answer given by Yahweh himself: millions of things happen every second that you and I know nothing about, from thunderbolts being sent in the Cook Islands to mountain goats giving birth in Tibet, but all of them are orchestrated by Almighty God. If ecological disasters and economic depressions occur at times, and we don't understand why, we shouldn't be surprised. We only found electricity a few years back, and we still can't figure out how to make even one living cell. As Job admits: "I have uttered what I did not understand, things too wonderful for me, which I did not know" (42:3).

Now, all of this is useful. These insights may help us cope with suffering ourselves, comfort others, and praise God through dark times. But in themselves, they are mere signposts into the fog, hints of an answer that has not yet come. The ultimate answer to suffering is not an argument, or an idea, but a person. Suffering's answer is Jesus.

Job hints at this. In Job 9:32-33, he expresses anguish that God is not a man, as we are, which means there's no arbiter between us and the Almighty. Then, in 23:3-7, he cries out for God's judgment throne to be within reach, so that he can have his case tried in court. Job believes his suffering would be answered if God could simply become man, relate to human suffering, and make his judgment throne available to humanity. Perhaps the writer to the Hebrews had this in mind when he said of Jesus:

> For we do not have a high priest who is unable to sympathize with our weaknesses, but one who in every respect has been tempted as we are, yet without sin. Let us then with confidence draw near to the throne of grace, that we may receive mercy and find grace to help in time of need. (Hebrews 4:15-16)

Imagine all humanity had a committee meeting to establish what God would have to go through, to truly understand human suffering. The poor would say he should be homeless, frequently hungry and constantly moving from place to place. The bereaved would say he should lose a parent, and perhaps a close friend as well. Outcasts would insist he face a major social stigma: accusations of illegitimacy, or drunkenness, or demon-possession. The abused might demand he face injustice, physical violence, ritual humiliation, abandonment and betrayal by those closest to him. I don't know what you would throw in—being murdered in his prime, perhaps, or facing extended torture and slow death. Maybe those who had felt the silence of heaven, like Job, would add that to the list, to form the most profound and wide-ranging suffering imagin-able. Then and only then, humanity might say, could God be regarded as being able to understand our suffering. Only if God had lived through the worst this life had to offer, and been perfect throughout, could we say he had provided Suffering's Answer.

THE SHADOW OF THE CROSS

My God, my God, why have you forsaken me?
(Psalm 22:1)

If Psalm 22 doesn't get your heart racing, you need to check your pulse. It gives insight into the suffering of Jesus like almost nothing else, it links together David and Christ with startling originality, and it proves beyond any doubt that God knows the future. In thirty-one verses, we are given detail after detail about the cross that no one but God could possibly have known, and yet the psalm still ends on a note of triumph rather than tragedy. The Messiah will suffer, it tells us, but he will be vindicated.

The psalm begins with a very famous line: "My God, my God, why have you forsaken me?" Originally written by David, probably while on the run from Saul, this deep cry of anguish is quoted in Aramaic by Jesus on the cross. This tells us firstly that David was prefiguring what would happen to Jesus. Quite unconsciously, David says that the Messiah, the true king and the true servant of Yahweh, will suffer. Most Jews were not expecting this.

Secondly, as the God-forsaken Savior cries out Psalm 22, he fulfills what happened to King David and so, very consciously, declares himself the Messiah. His suffering is exactly what an Israelite should expect if they had read their Old Testament properly.

To the crowds jeering at him on the cross, Jesus being strung up and humiliated proved he was not Israel's Savior. With his quotation of Psalm 22:1, however, Jesus offers proof that he was. Presumably anyone could quote David as they were dying, and claim the title Messiah. But as the psalm progresses, we notice links between David and Christ that could not possibly have happened except by the power and knowledge of God, since they involved numerous other people's choices. Taken together, they demonstrate that Jesus was right: he was the Son of David, he was Israel's Messiah, he was the King of the Jews (as, ironically, the piece of wood above his head declared), and he would be vindicated by God after his suffering.

David describes a crowd of scoffers:

> All who see me mock me; they make mouths at me;
> they wag their heads; "He trusts in the Lord; let him
> deliver him; let him rescue him, for he delights in him!"
> (Psalm 22:7-8)

Jump forward a thousand years, and you find this prophecy fulfilled exactly:

> And those who passed by derided him, wagging their heads ... So also the chief priests, with the scribes and elders, mocked him, saying, "He saved others; he cannot save himself. He is the King of Israel ... He trusts in God; let God deliver him now, if he desires him." (Matthew 27:39-43)

The idea of a righteous king of Israel going through intense pain and anguish would have been very surprising to people, but David gives no room for doubt:

> I am poured out like water, and all my bones are out of joint ... my tongue sticks to my jaws; you lay me in the dust of death. (Psalm 22:14-15)

David prophesied a type of persecution involving the dislocation of bones, intense thirst, and ultimately death. He could not have known that the Christ would experience all three, and he would not have known what to make of it if he did, since a dead Messiah was as unthinkable as a square circle. Furthermore, if you look carefully, when Jesus said "I thirst" (Jn. 19:28) and was given wine mixed with vinegar, it was not so much a statement of fact as a statement of fulfillment, both of this prophecy and of another of David's suffering psalms:

> They gave me poison for food, and for my thirst they gave me sour wine to drink. (Psalm 69:21)

Jesus was the king in the line of David, so he experienced all the sufferings David talked about. Even to death.

David describes the very details of Jesus' suffering: evildoers gathered round him who have "pierced [his] hands and feet" (Ps. 22:16). This gives me the shivers, because it was written not just a thousand years before Jesus was crucified—his hands and feet pierced with six-inch metal spikes—but five hundred years before crucifixion was even invented. No form of execution known at that time involved pierced hands and feet. Two verses later, David says that his tormentors "divide my garments among them, and for my clothing they cast lots" (Ps. 22:18). David, incredibly, predicts a method of execution where the victim is naked, states what happens to the clothes Jesus wore on the night of his betrayal, and the decisions made and games played by Roman soldiers not yet born. Psalm 22 holds an array of jarring and wonderful predictions that testify to the sovereignty and foreknowledge of the God who had already planned the cross.

All of these prophecies, though, are not the main point of the psalm. For that, we need to look at the ending, where the vindication of both Israel's King and Israel's God are announced, and the worship of the nations is promised:

> All the ends of the earth shall remember and turn to the LORD, and all the families of the nations shall worship before you. For kingship belongs to the LORD, and he rules over the nations ... they shall come and proclaim his righteousness to a people yet unborn, that he has done it. (Psalm 22:27-31)

Astounding. David prophesies that, through the suffering of the king, the ends of the earth will turn to Yahweh, and the families of the nations will worship him, in fulfillment of the promise to Abraham and in prediction of the great commission. What started off as a lament about being forgotten has turned into an anthem about being remembered, and the psalm fittingly ends with the promise that people not yet born will celebrate that "he has done it."

That's you. You fulfill Psalm 22 every time you praise God on your own, every time you break bread with other believers, every time you talk about Jesus to those who don't yet know him. Psalm 22 is fulfilled very time you proclaim that "he has done it."

iii
—

SINS FORGIVEN

Purge me with hyssop, and I shall
be clean; wash me, and I shall be
whiter than snow. Let me hear joy and
gladness; let the bones that you have
broken rejoice. Hide your face from my
sins, and blot out all my iniquities.
(Psalm 51:7-9)

Whiter than snow. Only two types of people could use a phrase like that, and only one of them could mean it. The first is a marketing executive for Procter and Gamble, and the second is someone who has experienced the swamping, sweeping forgiveness of Yahweh. I have been both, so I know the first is a rather silly exaggeration to sell washing powder. The second, on the other hand, is one of the most profound realities in the universe.

I'm sure there's a wide variety of people reading this book, with a whole range of sins in our pasts, but I doubt many have committed both adultery and murder in the last couple of weeks. King David had. In 2 Samuel 11-12, we read of David breaking eight of the ten commandments, and yet here he is, praying to Yahweh for restoration, and using phrases like "clean," "whiter than snow," "joy and gladness," and "rejoice." You might think him utterly audacious or deluded, but no. In fact, he understands Yahweh's forgiveness better than we do.

At a common-sense level, it just doesn't seem right, because we forgive people proportionately to the crime: if someone steps on my foot, no problem, but to forgive a rapist or a war criminal is something else. Yahweh doesn't work like we do, though. Every sin is an act of idolatry, and every forgiven sin requires God to be overwhelmingly gracious. Therefore David has every reason to think that God will forgive him—not because his sin is acceptable, but because his God is merciful. That's how grace works. Grace is based on God's character, not on ours. And it involves the *total* eradication of *every* sin we repent of.

The word-pictures David uses are his attempts to explain quite how dramatic this is. Take the phrase "whiter than snow," for example. I am writing this book in Atlantic Canada in February, and the province is basically one giant snowdrift. It was hardly snowing when I got home last night, though, so as I drove up my road, the car left a pair of dirty brown tracks behind me, like scars on the otherwise pure white landscape. Our sins are like that: dirty smears that taint the world we live in and they are painfully obvious to others. When I got up this morning, those tracks were rendered completely invisible by a perfect blanket of fresh snow that had fallen overnight. It looked like the road had been ironed; not only had my tracks been covered, but you would never be able to find them even if you wanted to. And if I drive out today and add new tire marks, they'll be as white as snow all over again tomorrow. And the day after that. And the day after that. The snow, like God's grace, falls new every morning, so no black marks—not even the massive ones left by snow plow vehicles, or the hideous messes we make of our relationships and finances—will withstand the whiteness of God's forgiveness.

Even those of us who can accept the snow picture might find David's next image troubling—how can such disgusting sin lead to so much joy that "broken bones rejoice" (Ps. 51:8)? Amazingly, the greater the sin we commit, the greater the joy at finding forgiveness, and the greater the love we feel towards the forgiver. Jesus makes this point in one of his most punchy parables:

> A certain moneylender had two debtors. One owed five hundred denarii, and the other fifty. When they could not pay, he canceled the debt of both. Now which of them will love him more? (Luke 7:41-42)

The more you have been forgiven, the happier you feel about it. So for a sinner to ask for forgiveness and not expect joy is like a parched man asking for a drink and not expecting refreshment. We're supposed to enjoy being forgiven.

Remarkably, David calls on Yahweh, not just to cover his sins, but to erase them completely (the same word is used of the creatures obliterated in the flood, for instance). "Blot out all my iniquities," David cries (Ps. 51:9), and this is exactly what God does. He remembers our sins no more, separating them from us like east from west. The very worst things we have done are destroyed, blotted out, never to reappear.

I don't know whether you've ever deleted a file on your computer, only to find that it's still hovering around in your deleted items, or backed up on your server, a year later. That is what sin can be like to us—we can forget it for a while, but it often bounces back into our minds and makes us feel guilty again. IT technicians tell me, however, that the way to get rid of files forever is to write over them with something else, replacing their content with new stuff. Once you've overwritten a file, the old version is completely removed from the hard drive. And that, wonder of wonders, is what sin is like to God. He overwrites our sins with his righteousness, and removes it completely from his memory. You see, our sins are not just canceled, leaving a blank instead of a debit. They are replaced, overwritten, leaving a credit instead of a debit. When God forgives you for your sins, he doesn't take you from negative one million to zero. He takes you from negative one million to a credit of one hundred million, decimating your sins forever and crediting you with righteousness.

All in all, forgiveness is pretty extraordinary. It deletes sins and delights sinners, leaving you, me, and David with clear records and clean hearts. Whether you're a murderer, a rapist, a pedophile or an idolater, forgiveness of sins is available if you repent. No wonder David sang so much.

iv

———

THE REALITY CHECK

We have all become like one who is
unclean, and all our righteous deeds
are like a polluted garment.
(Isaiah 64:6)

I have good news for you: you're far worse than you think.

To most people, that would probably sound like bad news. Most people want to think that they are fairly good, and don't usually welcome anyone telling them otherwise. But in some situations, discovering that you are far worse than you think can be excellent news. A child struggling at school may consider themselves to be stupid, but good news comes in the form of a dyslexia diagnosis. Understanding the real cause of a problem, however bad, brings the hope of a solution.

When it comes to our standing before God, we need an accurate assessment of ourselves. Just as we wouldn't mess around with an oncologist telling us we've got cancer, so we should not mess around with the living God. There will come a day when every one of us will stand before King Jesus and be answerable for our actions (2 Cor. 5:10), and on that day, there will be nowhere to hide, and no way to argue our way out of our mistakes. So finding out now that we are far worse than we thought is actually a good thing. It means we will not come unstuck when we stand before the judge of heaven and earth.

The evangelist Phil Moore refers to this reality check as the Simon Cowell moment. In the UK television show *X Factor* and its American counterpart, *American Idol*, showbiz hopefuls from all around the country audition for the chance to become famous and secure a record deal at the end of the series. Unfortunately, many of the contestants who appear on the show possess an inflated view of their musical ability. Some of them are simply appalling and yet have no idea how bad they sound, perhaps as a result of an enthusiastic family, a shower with generous acoustics, and the odd fact that none of us truly hear ourselves as we sound to others. Blissfully ignorant, these poor contestants then sing on television sounding like strangled sheep, all the while believing they are Beyoncé reborn.

Then they face Simon Cowell. After their performance, the feisty record producer gives them a blunt and often withering review, in which the insults fly and the showbiz hopeful comes crashing back to earth. While the whole thing is dramatized for entertainment, adding to the embarrassment, the main reason the contestants look so crushed is that they encounter a sudden reality check. To their ears and compared to their friends and their family, they sound fantastic—but now, with the world watching and in front of the only man who really matters, they are shown to be rather less talented than they thought.

Jesus, of course, is no Simon Cowell. He judges to bring justice, not humiliation; the driving force behind his judgments is expensive grace, not cheap laughs. Yet from our point of view, as ordinary folks with an unjustifiably high opinion of our righteousness, the experience will be much the same. Compared with our family, our friends, in our little world—in which we judge others by their actions and ourselves by our intentions—we may seem very righteous indeed. But on that day, with heaven watching and in front of the only One who really matters, we will be shown to be rather less righteous than we thought.

Isaiah's wonderful phrase sums up our natural state: "all our righteous deeds are like a polluted garment." To be honest, the translation here slightly softens the original, which pictures menstrual rags, soiled, filthy scraps of material, worthy only of being thrown away or burned. Compared to one another, our "righteous deeds," our very best efforts, might gain us brownie points, but compared to God, they are like a used sanitary towel. A sheep seems very white when compared to the rest of the farmyard, but put it in a snowy field and it looks decidedly yellow.

How, then, can this be good news? If our best efforts are useless, then what is the point of doing anything? Two things need to be said here. Firstly, Isaiah is talking about the righteous deeds of people without God: people who have continually sinned (Is. 64:5) and who do not call on his name (Is. 64:7). So we need not conclude that there is no way, ever, for people to please God. Instead, we see that pleasing God is impossible without trusting in him for help (Heb. 11:6). If we know that the Simon Cowell moment is coming, we are far more likely to call out to God for rescue.

The second thing is far more wonderful; we require a righteousness that is not our own. Here's the logic: if our righteous deeds are woefully inadequate (Is. 64:6), yet many people are still destined to be counted righteous (Is. 53:11), then *that righteousness must come from somewhere*. If you told your child that they were going to get 4000 metres up Mont Blanc, but they had no chance of climbing it, then they would tremble with excitement. They would know you'd booked a train ticket or perhaps a cable car. In the same way, God promises righteousness is available. This, coupled with the fact that my good deeds don't get me anywhere, indicates that righteousness will come to me from beyond myself, and that my standing before God will be based on the actions of someone else. Someone better.

But that is another story.

———

THE ARM OF YAHWEH

Who has believed what he has heard
from us? And to whom has the arm of
the LORD been revealed?
(Isaiah 53:1)

Four years ago, my friend Chris shot me in the face. We were in a friend's flat, in the kitchen, and he pointed a BB gun at me and pulled the trigger. He claims that he didn't think there was a pellet in it; whether or not that's true, there certainly was a bullet. A small, hard plastic ball hit me in the cheek at point-blank range, and it was extremely painful. Unknown to us, a man in the car park below our window had seen the whole thing—Chris pointing a gun at me and firing, then me reeling in pain and shouting, "You shot me in the face!"—and had called the police. The police took the threat seriously, and arrived at the flat at 3 a.m., bursting into my friend's bedroom through the fire exit in full riot gear. Half asleep and very confused, my friend had no idea why they kept asking him where the gun was. When he finally realized they must have mistaken his BB gun for a real one, he picked it up to show them, and was greeted with three rifles pointed at him to cries of "Drop the gun! Drop the gun!" The police finally accepted that it was a toy, but not before they had scared the living daylights out of everybody. They had come prepared for violent confrontation, and were quite disorientated when it turned out to be something else.

Isaiah's confusion and astonishment in the verse above may have been similar to the officers'. Isaiah's words express complete amazement at what he can see: "Who has believed it? To whom has it been revealed?" These are the questions of someone who has received revelation from God, but cannot quite bring himself to believe it yet. They are the questions of someone who knows that "the arm of Yahweh" means destruction and warfare and yet has just heard from God that his arm will include his own suffering and his sacrificial death. Not surprisingly, Isaiah can't quite square the circle.

You see, "the arm of Yahweh" always meant blood and judgment. In Exodus 6:6, God promised deliverance by his outstretched arm, and within weeks there came a series of plagues that make the film *Outbreak* look like a tea party. When the phrase next appears, the scene is more reminiscent of *Braveheart*, as an entire army gets wiped out in front of Israelites singing, "Terror and dread fall upon them; because of the greatness of your arm, they are still as a stone" (Ex. 15:16). So when Isaiah 52:10 promises, Yahweh "has bared his holy arm before the eyes of all the nations," you could be forgiven for thinking that the war to end all wars was coming. But that is not what happens.

Instead, Isaiah describes the arm of Yahweh as a *servant*. As his lens comes into focus in Isaiah 52:13 – 53:12, we see a servant so physically disfigured that you cannot tell what his face looks like: a man of sorrows, despised by other people, the sort of person that you hide your face from and pretend you haven't seen, like the toothless addict who asks you for money outside the bank. Who has believed it? To whom has the arm of Yahweh been revealed?

Looking on at this strange scene of a battered servant with whom no one made eye contact, Isaiah couldn't help spluttering in disbelief. Remember the riot police at my friend's flat? Based on their history and experience—when you hear about someone being shot, it usually means a violent showdown is approaching—the police were shocked to find a person in pyjamas carrying a plastic pistol. In the same way, based on his history and experience, Isaiah assumed the arm of Yahweh meant a violent showdown. He was shocked to find instead a suffering servant carrying a Roman cross. On that cross, however, was a victory more profound and everlasting than any other, one that astonished people then and bamboozles them now. For on that cross, once and for all, God bared his holy arm in the sight of all the nations, and ground wickedness into the dust.

This is one of Scripture's most surprising twists. The arm of Yahweh was still working rescue for God's people, but in a totally new way. Destruction, blood and judgment were still there, but the destruction was that of transgressions, the blood that of a sacrifice, and the judgment poured out on the only person who didn't deserve it. God's arm was brandished and ready for battle, but the fight was not with sinful people but with sin itself. The battleground of the whole scene was Jesus: the fist and the punching-bag, the Servant King, the arm of Yahweh in human form. But in the end, the result was the same: victory for God and the spoils of battle to his Son (Is. 53:12).

Arm of Yahweh, one: sin and death, nil.

A NEW SPIRIT

> I will sprinkle clean water on you,
> and you shall be clean from all your
> uncleannesses, and from all your idols I
> will cleanse you. And I will give you a
> new heart, and a new spirit I will put
> within you. And I will remove the heart
> of stone from your flesh and give you a
> heart of flesh. And I will put my Spirit
> within you, and cause you to walk in my
> statutes and be careful to obey my rules.
> (Ezekiel 36:25-27)

I'll be honest with you: I find reading the prophets very hard work sometimes. I've been reading them in my devotional times while writing this book, and again and again I have been confronted with long passages promising nothing but judgment. They can be quite depressing and a bit overwhelming. How are we supposed to respond to endless chapters ex-

plaining how Israel, Judah, and pretty much everyone else will
be destroyed because of disobedience? What am I meant to
learn from the ongoing cycle of sin and punishment? The sinfulness of humanity, obviously; the holiness of God, certainly.
However, I cannot help but respond to the prophecies of
judgment like an emperor penguin responds to the Antarctic
winter—with persistent endurance and gritted teeth, waiting
for the light to break.

And the light always breaks. That's the beauty of the
prophets. They are so sure of Yahweh's unceasing and steadfast
love that they know things won't always be like this. Even when
Israel wars against Judah, kings worship false gods, and idols
and phallic symbols stand "on every high hill and under every
spreading tree" (1 Kgs. 14:23, NIV), Yahweh remains true. He
still keeps his covenant with Abraham. So the prophets know
that, ultimately, God is going to change things. God will have
to initiative this change, because the people keep flunking it.
And some fairly dramatic changes to the way humanity works
is certainly required, because even God's chosen people don't
seem to be able to obey him, let alone everyone else. But the alternative—humanity being left to their own devices, abandoned
by God and rotting in sin—is unthinkable. God is faithful.

Welcome to Ezekiel's world. This priest-turned-prophet had
the tough task of speaking to the Jews in exile, after centuries
of decline and disobedience had led to them being invaded,
besieged, taken captive and marched across the Middle East to
Babylon, in modern day Iraq. The ungodliness of the people
is shocking: Israel and Judah prostituted themselves to false
gods, placed idols in the temple and worshiped the sun; abominations abounded. Ezekiel's book is filled with judgment on

Judah for their sins, some so graphic it found its way into *Pulp Fiction* (fire, vengeance, slaughter, famine, disease …), and to top it all off, the Babylonians destroy the temple in 587 BC. All in all, it is a fairly dark hour for the people of God.

But the darkest hour comes just before the dawn. Just as we conclude that human beings will never walk in God's ways on their own, Ezekiel reveals Yahweh's astonishing answer: human beings will indeed never walk in God's ways on their own, so they will be given completely new hearts and spirits. I will sprinkle clean water on you, Yahweh says. I will take out your old heart and give you a new one. No longer will you be hard like stone, but soft like flesh; in fact, I am going to put my Spirit inside you, and he will cause you to follow my ways like you've never done before. I am going to take the initiative, and it will change you forever.

In spite of the way we often think, you and I remain incapable of pleasing God without the Holy Spirit living in us. It's not that it's difficult; it's impossible. Telling me to walk in God's ways with my natural heart of stone is like telling an apple tree to produce oranges: the apple tree can strain, and attend an accountability group, and make a hundred resolutions, but it will never produce oranges unless it gets given completely new DNA. We're like that. Our hearts of stone, try as we might, won't produce obedience to God; instead we need completely new DNA—the Spirit of God within us, in every cell, so that we may live to please him. Without the Spirit, the Christian life would be impossible, a futile life of straining and accountability groups and broken resolutions. With the Spirit, though, we produce godliness as naturally as an orange tree makes oranges.

Lots of people are baffled by this, because it sounds like there's nothing we can do by our own effort; it's all a question of being given something by God. Yes. That's exactly what Ezekiel 36 is about; the history of Israel is a diary of life without the Spirit, and it doesn't work. Only the Spirit's work in us can producing God-honoring behavior. This is where Jesus was coming from when he announced to an equally baffled Pharisee:

> Truly, truly, I say to you, unless one is born of water and the Spirit, he cannot enter the kingdom of God. That which is born of the flesh is flesh, and that which is born of the Spirit is spirit. (John 3:5-6)

That's not to say that obedience is automatic—we may resist or ignore our new DNA—but obedience isn't difficult, either. In fact, it comes naturally as we walk with him. I cannot count the number of people I know who become Christians and then, without ever being told what to do, stop doing drugs and swearing and getting drunk and sleeping around—not by straining, or by being threatened, but by walking in the Spirit. That's because God gives us new DNA, a new heart and a new spirit, not a new rulebook or a new method. It's because he makes us want different things, not just strive for them; he gives us new desires, not just new disciplines.

Ezekiel, who lived six centuries before the Holy Spirit came to live in people like this, would have loved to be where you are today. He would have relished the chance to be given a new spirit, like you have, and he would have daydreamed of what might happen if the whole of Israel was given one. No more idolatry, no more abominations, no more prophecies of judgment, just a glorious story of new creation and delighted obedience. The light always breaks.

A NEW COVENANT

"The days are coming," declares the
LORD, "when I will make a new covenant
with the people of Israel and with the
people of Judah … I will put my law
in their minds and write it on their
hearts. I will be their God, and they
will be my people. No longer they·teach
their neighbor, or say to one another,
'Know the LORD,' because they will all
know me, from the least of them to the
greatest," declares the LORD. "For I
will forgive their wickedness and will
remember their sins no more."
(Jeremiah 31:31-34, NIV)

By my reckoning, Jeremiah had a pretty awful job. He had to
prophesy at length about the destruction of Jerusalem while
he was still living there, knowing that the darkest moment

in Israel's history was coming right around the corner like an unseen juggernaut. He cried himself dry knowing Israel wasn't going to listen to a word he said in warning. In the circumstances, what's surprising is not how distressed he felt, but how hopeful.

Jeremiah 31 contains, in many ways, the most profound and sweeping expression of hope in the entire Old Testament. It speaks of something that, in the context, seemed spectacularly improbable: a new covenant to replace the law of Moses. It's hard to grasp how unlikely this felt, because not many things in our culture are as old as the law of Moses was then. The first covenant was older then than the English language is now. Not only that, but God had established the covenant with Moses, and confirmed it with a whole array of terrifying signs and wonders. To announce a new covenant would be like predicting the Faroe Islands were going to win the World Cup, or that the Giant Panda was going to overtake the beetle as the world's most common animal. No way.

Yet Jeremiah prophesied a new covenant anyway. And he prophesied it with passion and excitement, sketching out for us how the new covenant will deal with every aspect of Israel's sinfulness in a perfect and everlasting way. I can picture him trying to explain what he can see, breathlessly describing it to his assistant: "Baruch, there's going to be a new covenant, not like the old one, but a new one, and the law won't be on tablets any more, it'll kind of be in people's hearts and minds, and it will be so well known that people won't even have to teach each other anymore, because everyone will know God, no matter who they are, because he'll forgive everyone's sins, in fact, he'll forgive them so utterly that he won't even remember them, and ..."

The covenant would be brand new, replacing the old one and making it obsolete, just as a new will overrides all previous ones. It will be written in people's hearts; they will *love* to keep God's law, not just *try* to keep it. It would be written in their minds as well, bringing their thoughts in line with God's thoughts. It would restore a depth of relationship that had long since been damaged by persistent rebellion. It would be all-encompassing, so that everyone could know God. It would involve the total forgiveness and forgetfulness of all of their sins, not just the covering of them through the sacrificial system.

Now let's jump forward to another Jewish prophet who saw destruction coming and wept over Jerusalem. He eats a meal with his friends, and as the meal comes to an end, something astonishing suddenly happens. He takes the cup, and announces, "This cup is the *new covenant* in my blood, which is poured out for you" (Lk. 22:20, NIV). We sometimes hear those words as a nice phrase to say before communion. But if we understand the story of the new covenant, like the disciples did, it quickly becomes clear that Jesus is going to the cross because he is initiating the new covenant. After six centuries of waiting, the new covenant Jeremiah prophesied arrives. As the writer to the Hebrews triumphantly puts it:

> Therefore [Christ] is the mediator of a new covenant, so that those who are called may receive the promised eternal inheritance, since a death has occurred that redeems them from the transgressions committed under the first covenant … as it is, he has appeared once for all at the end of the ages to put away sin by the sacrifice of himself. (Hebrews 9:15, 26)

The old covenant was holy and good, but it dealt with sin in daily chunks. Every day, a priest had to do his duties and make sacrifices, which served as an ongoing reminder that Israel's sin had still not been fully dealt with. The new covenant, by contrast, required only one sacrifice—the "once for all" sacrifice of Jesus—and no other.

There never will be another sacrifice, either. This serves as decisive proof that sins have been completely wiped out, and that Jeremiah's new covenant has come. Gospel preaching will never be the same again:

> ... our sufficiency is from God, who has made us sufficient to be ministers of a new covenant, not of the letter but of the Spirit. For the letter kills, but the Spirit gives life. (2 Corinthians 3:5-6)

THE STONE AND THE SON

> And in the days of those kings the
> God of heaven will set up a kingdom
> that shall never be destroyed, nor
> shall the kingdom be left to another
> people. It shall break in pieces all
> these kingdoms and bring them to an
> end, and it shall stand forever, just
> as you saw that a stone was cut from a
> mountain by no human hand, and that it
> broke in pieces the iron, the bronze,
> the clay, the silver and the gold.
> (Daniel 2:44-45)

Kingdoms come and kingdoms go. From God's viewpoint, it must look ridiculous when earthly empires believe they will exist forever; it is as if a group of aphids was to celebrate their eternal dominance over a tree. History teems with kings who get too big for their boots and are clobbered by Yahweh as a result—Pharaoh, Sennacherib, Nebuchadnezzar, Herod—and when that happens, we see one of two outcomes. Either the empire is destroyed altogether (when did you last meet an Assyrian, or a Babylonian?), or it is taken over by others. World history tells a consistent story: no kingdoms last forever.

Which all makes the prophecy of Daniel 2 completely outrageous. The next few centuries, Daniel says, are going to follow the normal pattern of human history: the current world power (Babylon) will be conquered by a new one (Persia), who will then be thrown down by a third (Greece), who will eventually be crushed by the military might of a fourth (Rome). But during the rule of the fourth empire, the God of heaven will set up another one, which will never be destroyed, and which will never be left to another people—"it shall stand for ever." That means it will be the only empire in history that neither gets wiped out nor passed to others. Bizarre.

The mystery doesn't stop there. "In the days of those kings" God will establish his kingdom. It's rather strange wording, isn't it? Normally, you only establish a kingdom by destroying the previous one. But Daniel doesn't say that. He says that God will found his empire in the midst of the existing one. It sounds like the everlasting kingdom is going to exist while a worldly empire remains apparently in charge.

It is also incredible that this should be prophesied by a Jew. Israel didn't look like very likely candidates to receive an everlasting kingdom. As Daniel recorded this prophecy, they were not even in control of their own country, let alone anyone else's. Worse: they were not even *in* their own country, but captives in Babylon, ruled by the very man Daniel explains the vision to. All in all, it sounds fairly ludicrous that Israel's

God will set up an everlasting kingdom that will outlast all the others.

Plenty of people in Daniel's day, and plenty in ours, made a living out of pretending they could tell people the meaning of dreams. Nebuchadnezzar's court was full of them, ancient Professor Trelawneys who claimed they knew what dreams meant. One day he decided to call them on it. He declared that they had to tell him not just what his dream meant, but what his dream was in the first place—and that if they couldn't, they would be torn limb from limb. You can imagine the panic: these horoscope writers were about to get found out as frauds, so they told the king their task was impossible, since God does not dwell with flesh. Into this arena steps Daniel, who promptly reveals that God does dwell with flesh, that he does reveal mysteries, and that God knows both what the king dreamt and what it meant. A random prophecy from an unknown person might not carry much weight. But telling the world's most powerful man what he dreamt last night, under threat of death, is weighty.

In the days of the fourth empire (the Romans), the God of heaven did indeed set up a kingdom. That kingdom did begin while another empire appeared to rule. It has, like the stone in Nebuchadnezzar's dream, broken other kingdoms in pieces and crushed them. It has outlasted any earthly kingdom, including the Romans. Two thousand years on, it stands strong. And this empire continues to expand and fill the earth, with new people groups being brought into it every year. You probably know it as the kingdom of God:

Have you never read in the Scriptures, "The *stone* that
the builders rejected has become the cornerstone; this
was the Lord's doing, and it is marvelous in our eyes"?
Therefore I tell you, *the kingdom of God* will be taken
away from you and given to a people producing its fruits.
And the one who falls on this *stone* will be *broken to pieces*;
and when it falls on anyone, it will crush him. (Matthew
21:42-44, my italics)

That's pretty bold. Jesus declares that his kingdom of preaching and healing and casting out demons is the stone that was
rejected, but will eventually break every worldly empire to
pieces. Jesus declares that his kingdom is the real fulfillment
of Daniel 2.

But bolder still, when we realize this teaching comes at the
end of a parable about God sending his Son to Israel, and Israel
rejecting and killing him. Now get this: in Hebrew, the word
for "stone" (*eben*) sounds almost exactly like the word for "son"
(*ben*). Jesus is making a very provocative pun. Fundamentally,
the rejected stone and the rejected son are one and the same:
Jesus. Yet this rejected Son, this rejected Stone, is finally going to
be vindicated. The Son is establishing an everlasting kingdom
that will stand forever, and crush all the others:

I saw in the night visions, and behold, with the clouds of
heaven there came *one like a son of man*, and he came to
the Ancient of Days and was presented before him. And
to him was given dominion and glory and a kingdom,
that all peoples, nations and languages should serve him;
his dominion is an everlasting dominion, which shall not

pass away, and his kingdom one that shall not be destroyed.
(Daniel 7:13-14, my italics)

Daniel was right. The Stone and the Son are one and the same.

THE SPIRIT POURED OUT

And it shall come to pass afterward, that
I will pour out my Spirit on all flesh;
your sons and daughters shall prophesy,
your old men shall dream dreams, and your
young men shall see visions. Even on the
male and female servants in those days I
will pour out my Spirit.
(Joel 2:28-29)

Christians often stop the gospel story in the wrong place. Frequently, the gospel is talked about as Creation — Fall — Crucifixion — Resurrection — Judgment, which involves jumping from Genesis 3 to Matthew 27 to Revelation 20, and skipping almost everything else. When people stop and think about it more carefully, they might include the life of Jesus(!) and perhaps even the history of Israel. In my limited experience, though, people almost always stop the tape on Easter Sunday and then fast forward to the return of Jesus. This may be because people aren't too sure what happens in between, or how relevant it all is to salvation. But in doing so, they miss one of the most thrilling bits, like a mountaineer so desperate to get home he fails to savor the summit. They miss the Spirit being poured out.

The prophet Joel didn't. Nor did Peter, who quoted Joel's words on the day of Pentecost in Acts 2, or Jesus, who spent most of his last hours talking about him (Jn. 14-16). Luke would be astonished that anyone could talk about Christianity without mentioning the Spirit, and would explain in detail how Pentecost changed everything. Paul would go further, and remind us that people without the Spirit don't even belong to Christ (Rom. 8:9). To the apostles, and to Jesus, the pouring out of the Holy Spirit represented one of the high points of the entire story, the bit that, quite literally, everybody was waiting for:

> And behold, I am sending the promise of my Father upon you. But stay in the city until you are clothed with power from on high. (Luke 24:49)

> John baptized with water, but you will be baptized with the Holy Spirit not many days from now ... You will receive power when the Holy Spirit has come upon you, and you will be my witnesses in Jerusalem and in all Judea and Samaria, and to the end of the earth. (Acts 1:5, 8)

> This Jesus God raised up, and of that we are all witnesses. Being therefore exalted at the right hand of God, and having received from the Father the promise of the Holy

> Spirit, he has poured out this that you yourselves are
> seeing and hearing. (Acts 2:32-33)

What is so important about the pouring out of the Holy Spirit? Let me suggest five things.

First, he is the Spirit of power. This is probably the major emphasis of the story in Luke-Acts. Jesus repeatedly promises power to his disciples, and Luke is then careful to show us the promise fulfilled, with healings, wonders spoken, buildings shaken, demons cast out and so on. At Pentecost, the age of power began, and that age continues—we can only accomplish God's mission if we are filled with God's power, just like a car can only run if it has been filled with fuel. The coming of the Spirit of power upon the church is one of the things Luke, and the early church he documents, got most excited about.

Second, he is the Spirit of purity, as we see in Jeremiah and Ezekiel. There's a good reason he gets referred to as the "Holy" Spirit—unholy and impure people like us get to be holy and pure people like God when we receive him. Galatians 5 is pretty blunt about this: if we walk in the Spirit, we will keep free from sin; our very own live-in life coach shows us how to please God. Prophets with a passion for holiness, like Jeremiah and Ezekiel, sat on the edge of their seats awaiting the Spirit of purity coming to God's people.

Third, he is the Spirit of possession. We know we belong to Christ how? When the Holy Spirit comes upon us.[1] The Holy Spirit is the seal God puts on all believers, the proof in our

---

1   This is especially significant in Paul's teaching, see for example Ephesians 1:13-14; Romans 8:14-17.

hearts that we are his children. He is the way we know that we are in Christ and Christ is in us. His seal also assures other people we belong to God; it was only when the Holy Spirit fell on Cornelius and his household that Peter was convinced they had been forgiven their sins and should be baptized. The Spirit functions as a sort of ID badge for Christians, a bit like circumcision did for the Jews. When you have the Spirit, you know for sure you are God's possession.

Fourth, he is the Spirit of presence. Of all people in the New Testament, Jesus was the most insistent on this: I go away for your good, he said, because when I do, I will send another helper to be with you (Jn. 16:7). This didn't sound like good news at first, but it turned out better than his disciples could possibly have imagined. Jesus sent the Holy Spirit, the one who would bring God's presence to millions of believers at once. In an age of Wi-Fi, you won't find many people pining for a dial-up connection. Consequently, with the presence of Jesus available everywhere at once, Spirit-filled believers do "even greater things" than he did (Jn. 14:12, NIV).

Fifth, he is the Spirit of prophecy. Joel longed for the day when "your sons and daughters shall prophesy." Both Peter and Paul were emphatic about it: when the Spirit comes, people prophesy. Not just prophets or experienced disciples, but sons and daughters, servants, the young, the old. Prophecy happens frequently in Acts when people receive the Spirit, and Paul even urges his most out-there charismatic church, Corinth, to eagerly desire to prophesy (1 Cor. 14:1). No doubt some people have gone too far, and made the use of certain gifts (like tongues or prophecy) the mark of salvation. But others have not gone far enough, and either neglected or decided not to pursue prophecy at all, for a variety of reasons. It has been my privilege to interact with many gifted prophets in the last few years, and Joel was right. When the Spirit comes, people will prophesy.

The pouring out of the Spirit was quite something. Don't stop the story in the wrong place. Don't act as if Scripture jumps from resurrection to return, and miss out the marvel of the indwelling, empowering, baptizing, filling, gift-giving Spirit. The Spirit of Pentecost is the Spirit of promise—Joel's Spirit of prophecy and Ezekiel's Spirit of purity and Jesus' Spirit of presence and Luke's Spirit of power and Paul's Spirit of possession—all rolled into one glorious package and poured out in one glorious person. So, as Paul urges:

> Do not get drunk with wine, for that is debauchery, but be filled with the Spirit, addressing one another in psalms and hymns and spiritual songs, singing and making melody to the Lord with your heart, giving thanks always and for everything to God the Father in the name of our Lord Jesus Christ, submitting to one another out of reverence for Christ. (Ephesians 5:18-21)

ACT FOUR

JESUS AND RESCUE

CONCERNING HIS SON

> Paul, a servant of Christ Jesus,
> called to be an apostle, set apart for
> the gospel of God, which he promised
> beforehand through his prophets in the
> holy Scriptures, concerning his Son,
> who was descended from David according
> to the flesh and was declared to be the
> Son of God in power according to the
> Spirit of holiness by his resurrection
> from the dead, Jesus Christ our Lord ...
> (Romans 1:1-4)

I don't think any verses in Scripture summarize the gospel better than Romans 1:1-4. Paul serves us espresso theology, the gospel with not a word wasted, and it may therefore cause a splutter or perhaps a headrush to those of us more used to drinking cappuccino or Americano. The Magna Carta contains over 4,000 words, and the Declaration of Independence, 1,321.

Lincoln's Gettysburg Address, famously brief, comes in at 267 words long. Yet here, Paul summarizes the greatest of all announcements in a mere forty Greek words. Enlivening and uplifting, Romans 1:1-4 is also extremely concentrated so, like any rich expresso, we're going to take it slow.

The news that Paul announces is not, and never has been, a new thing. Christianity is the fulfillment of an old thing, the climax of thousands of promises and prophecies given "beforehand" through dozens of people across at least forty centuries. In a well-written whodunnit there always comes a moment at the end when the detective explains how the murder was committed, and how all the puzzling strands come together in one solution. Paul says the gospel is like that: the dénouement, where all the various strands you had been wondering about—exodus and exile, priests and sacrifices, kings and servants, suffering and victory—come together into one mind-blowing solution.

Paul's whole sentence pivots on the next phrase, "concerning his Son." You cannot overstate the centrality of Jesus to the gospel. Ultimately, God's gospel is not "concerning his salvation," or "concerning his love," but concerning his Son. Remember, here Paul is opening a letter packed with great detail about justification by faith, being in Christ, life in the Spirit, and so on. Paul's passion overflows about these things. But they, in themselves, are not what the gospel is about. These truths move like planets in orbit: large and important in themselves, but still revolving around a massive center of gravity far bigger than themselves. In the middle of this theological solar system stands the Son: his identity, his life, his death, his resurrection, and his reign. The gospel hinges on Jesus.

Next we read that Jesus was fully human: "descended from David according to the flesh." We might be tempted to think this a bit peripheral to a gospel summary but, to Paul, Jesus' descent from David holds huge significance. It means at least three things. It means Jesus was a *man*, a real person who had a descent "according to the flesh," with real parents and ancestors. It means he was a *Jewish* man, circumcised and law-keeping, able to fulfill God's promises to Israel. And it means he was the *rightful king*, the heir of the throne of David, the one prophesized to rule over the nations on behalf of Yahweh. The gospel is about a man.

The gospel is about a man "declared to be the Son of God in power." What a statement. This Jewish construction worker with a northern accent, who had brothers and sisters, who had a job and paid taxes and went to the toilet and slept and ate fish and cried and cracked jokes and washed feet, was declared to be the Son of God in power. If you've lost a sense of how shocking this is, just explain it to an orthodox Jew for a minute, and you'll quickly realize how controversial it originally sounded. This man from Nazareth was God's Messiah, described later as "God over all" (Romans 9:5). The Son of God in power.

So how did this declaration happen? Paul says it happened "according to the Spirit of holiness, by his resurrection from the dead." The third member of the Trinity joins the scene, as he loudly announces to the world the authority now given to the Son, by his resurrection from the dead. Jesus was not raised by a medium, a séance or an Ouija board, or any other unclean spirit; he was raised according to the Spirit of holiness, in all his perfection and purity. The resurrection, fundamentally, was the Father's proclamation of the Son's lordship by the Spirit's power. If you worry that the Trinity is an impractical and theoretical idea, you just need to look at the empty tomb.

The result of all these things is summed up in the phrase "Jesus Christ our Lord." Books could be written on those four words, but the headline is clear: Jesus is the "Christ," the promised king of Israel; he is "Lord," the ruler of the whole world; and he is "our" Lord, the one whom *we* can know and praise and love and follow.

The gospel is primarily a person, not an event. It's not "of me, concerning my salvation"—as if I occupy the center of the universe—but "of God, concerning his Son." The front pages of the early morning newspapers scream "Gospel of God!" accompanied by a picture of a Middle-Eastern carpenter. The subtitle elaborates with three simple words: "Concerning his Son."

THE KINGDOM OF GOD IS AT HAND

"The time is fulfilled, and the
kingdom of God is at hand; repent and
believe in the gospel."
(Mark 1:15)

If you had asked Jesus to summarize the gospel of God, he would have said simply that the kingdom of God was at hand. If you had asked him what to do about it, he would have told you to repent and believe the gospel. If you had asked him what it meant, he would have shown you with his actions and told you story after story. Actually, for the three years he traveled around Galilee and Judea, that's pretty much what he did.

Many Christians haven't been quite sure what to make of this. Removed from a Jewish context, and without any understanding of what "the kingdom of God" means, it is easy for modern Westerners to get confused. If you rummage through your New Testament, though, you'll find that not only did Jesus preach the kingdom in his earthly ministry, but he also spent the days after the resurrection explaining it, and the apostles followed his example, preaching and demonstrating it wherever they went. From time to time you hear the claim that "Jesus preached the kingdom and the church preached Jesus." But to imply Jesus and the church preached different things is complete rubbish. Both Jesus and the early church announced the same gospel—the kingdom of God is at hand—in word and action, with the life and death of Jesus firmly at the center. We may have since got muddled up about it, or dropped it altogether, but the apostles knew it.

Some statements just look wrong without an exclamation mark: "Mildred just had triplets." "Which means the murderer was none other than ... Lord Bunfastley." "Look, the lost treasure of the Sierra Madre."[1] We announce statements like these, not just drop them lightly into conversation. "The kingdom of God is near!" (NLT) deserves announcing with a loudspeaker and neon lights. "The kingdom is near!" brings to its conclusion centuries of waiting, and had an immediate impact on the communities that first heard it because they knew the backstory.

But what does it mean? Well, the good news in the Old Testament, essentially, was that Israel's God reigned supreme, and all other gods, rulers and nations did not. Although faithful Jews trusted that God ruled, it often didn't look that way. Israel (through its own sin) frequently found itself under

---

1 I owe these statements to the playwright and comedian John Finnemore, in private correspondence.

the boot of a foreign power. They yearned for a day when all people would be able to see that Yahweh was in charge, as he returned to Jerusalem to destroy his enemies and bring restoration to his people:

> How beautiful upon the mountains are the feet of him who brings good news, who publishes peace, who brings good news of happiness, who publishes salvation, who says to Zion, "Your God reigns." The voice of your watchmen—they lift up their voice; together they sing for joy; for eye to eye they see the return of the LORD to Zion. (Isaiah 52:7-8)

"The kingdom of God is at hand," then, acted as a proclamation that this was now happening. After hundreds of years of waiting, Yahweh was returning to his people, his enemies were going to be crushed, and his reign (which you could equally call his kingdom) drew close.

So far, so good. That was what the Jews meant, and that was what Jesus meant. However, it quickly became clear that Jesus' idea of what these things looked like didn't match what any Jew expected. God's reign would not be accepted by everyone; in fact, lots of people (including the religious leaders) would reject it. The enemies crushed included sickness, Satan, demonic powers and sin, but not Roman soldiers. Worst of all, the return of Yahweh would mean judgment for Israel and her temple, not exaltation. The prophet from Nazareth was turning the popular notion of the kingdom of God on its head through the things he did and the stories he told.

Outsiders in Israel—lepers, deaf and blind people, those who couldn't walk, even the demonized—were being healed, so that they could fully participate in the community of God. The "worst" sinners, such as crooked tax collectors and sexually immoral women, were being welcomed and invited to dinner. People with no place in Israel at all, such as Samaritans and Romans, found themselves included, and (worse) held up as examples for good Jews to imitate. Jesus knew what he was doing. In each unexpected action, he signified that the kingdom of God was much wider than anyone had realized, and that it was going to incorporate more than just Israel.

And then the stories … sons who say they'll obey but then don't (like good Jews) lose out to sons who say they won't obey but then do (like sinners). The son who comes back from the foreign pigsty gets invited to the banquet, while the son who has been there the whole time sits and sulks. You shouldn't love just your Jewish neighbors, but everybody, even Samaritans. People who turn up at the vineyard late (like Gentiles) will get the same privileges as those who've been there all day (like Jews). God's banquet will be full of people you would never expect: outsiders, the poor, the sick, unthinkables from the highways and hedges. The rich will be poor, the poor will be rich, the first will be last and the last will be first. And so it goes on, as Jesus hammers a new understanding of the kingdom into his listeners. The kingdom of God is at hand, but it's not what you thought.

Of course, that picture of the kingdom flummoxed people. No one could figure out how Gentiles could ever be included in God's people without being made clean. No one could understand what healing and casting out demons had to do with anything. No one had any idea why God would want lepers and tax collectors and prostitutes in his empire. From this side of the cross, however, we have the privilege of seeing how the kingdom Jesus described came to be. We can see that God's rule is shown even more emphatically by saving Gentiles than by destroying them; we can see that Jesus had a plan to make even the most disgusting sinner right with God, whatever their race; and we can see that Yahweh is sovereign not just over politics, but over sickness, sin, Satan, demons and even death. The kingdom of God is at hand—repent, and believe the gospel.

REGENERATION

Now there was a man of the Pharisees
named Nicodemus, a ruler of the Jews.
This man came to Jesus by night and said
to him, "Rabbi, we know that you are a
teacher come from God, for no one can
do these signs that you do unless God is
with him." Jesus answered him, "Truly,
truly, I say to you, unless one is born
again he cannot see the kingdom of God."
(John 3:1-3)

I have always found it a bit peculiar when people ask if I am a
"born again" Christian. Is there another kind? It's like asking
someone if they're a "medicine-dispensing" pharmacist or a
"music-making" guitar player. The label "born again Christian"
implies two sorts of disciple, those who are born again and
those who aren't. But Jesus doesn't see it that way. He says that
if you're not born again, you cannot see the kingdom at all.

It's an extraordinary statement. You can't go back inside your mother and go through the whole thing again, can you? It's a crazy idea. Yet there it is, on the lips of God himself. If you want to be in God's kingdom, you have to be "born again" (or, as theologians often say, "regenerated"). You have to be made from scratch by the Spirit of God.

Jesus' teaching flows straight from his true understanding of human sinfulness, and the size of the problem it presents. To many Jews like Nicodemus, the answer to the problem of human sin was obedience to God's law and faithfulness to his covenant. To Gentiles, human sin wasn't that much of a problem; their gods didn't require holiness from people, and most of their gods weren't even holy themselves. Jesus, however, knew that Gentiles had misunderstood God and that Jews had misunderstood people. He knew that there was a massive problem: God is holy, we are not, and no amount of effort could make up the difference. The solution was not to try again, or even to start again, but to be born again.

In the cult sci-fi film, *The Matrix*, the main character Neo lives his life in a computer-generated dreamworld, in which everything looks and feels pretty much like the real world does today. In reality, however, he is permanently suspended in pink fluid along with millions of others, being harvested for electricity by a bunch of machines fooling his brain not to notice. He cannot think his way out of this dreamworld, neither can he try and earn his way out of it. The fake world exerts too much power. Instead, he has to be (almost literally) born again, removed from the pink fluid capsule and introduced to the real world for the first time. His muscles need building, his worldview needs completely reconstructing, and his relationships need totally transforming to adjust to the new reality. He finds it completely disorientating, and so do we. But being regenerated is the only way he can be saved out of captivity and into a free reality.

God's in the business of that sort of radical re-making of people through the gospel, by his Holy Spirit. We can't enter the kingdom without rebirth, because the sinful nature we inherit, and the false worldview we have lived with for so long, exert too much power. If sin was ultimately a problem with our thinking, we could solve it by thinking new thoughts; if it was ultimately a problem with our feelings, we could experience new emotions; if it was ultimately a problem with our actions, we could do new things. All other religions and secular worldviews believe that one of these three is the answer to humanity's problems. But they're all wrong. Sin is ultimately a problem with our being, our very nature, so it can only be solved by becoming a new creature. A totally new sort-of-something.

Which is what Jesus announces to a startled Nicodemus in the middle of the night. Jesus was proclaiming a reality that the prophets had talked about for centuries (check out Ezekiel 36). That doesn't mean it wasn't shocking, though. Hearing that your very being needs to change to enter the kingdom, and that this only takes place by the power of God's Spirit, is a bit overwhelming. Yet it is also the foundation stone of the good news: we enter the kingdom on God's initiative, and get given a completely new nature by him. Or, as Paul put it: "if anyone is in Christ, he is a new creation. The old has passed away; behold, the new has come" (2 Cor. 5:17).

This language of new creation is immensely powerful. Remember, in the beginning, God spoke light into being and there was light, shining in the darkness, brought about by the word of God through the Spirit of God (Gen. 1:1-2). Then, as John's Gospel opens, we hear almost identical phrases being used to describe the new creation that starts with Jesus:

> *In the beginning* was the *Word* … In him was life, and that life was *the light* of men. *The light shines in the darkness*, and the darkness has not overcome it. (John 1:1, 4-5, my italics)

If you're a disciple of Jesus, you're part of his completely new creation. You are not simply the "old you" who has learned to think, or feel, or act differently. You are a new creature, and you think and feel and act differently because of who you are. You have been regenerated, made new, born again by the Spirit of God.

CHRIST CRUCIFIED

> For Jews demand signs and Greeks seek
> wisdom, but we preach Christ crucified,
> a stumbling block to Jews and folly to
> Gentiles, but to those who are called,
> both Jews and Greeks, Christ the power
> of God and the wisdom of God.
> (1 Corinthians 1:22-24)

The cross of Jesus is a gory story of shame and pain, violence and silence. It is almost impossible to speak too strongly about it. If it doesn't bother us, then we probably haven't thought it through. Like the Holocaust or the Rwandan genocide, remaining indifferent to the crucifixion is completely inappropriate. You may shrug your shoulders at Buddha, or even Muhammad, but as soon as you stop and think about Christ crucified, you cannot avoid a strong reaction. That's the whole point.

Extreme reactions to the cross take many forms. Many people think the idea that the suffering of a good man could be of any value is the dumbest thing they've ever heard. These days, you will find lots of people get very angry with the cross, because it implies that their greed and sexual immorality and pride might require punishment. Still others will see Jesus' death as one of history's great tragedies, as a good teacher gets cut down in his prime by the wicked powers-that-be. Some, wonderfully, find their lives turned upside-down by the love and holiness they encounter there. One thing people do not do, however, is listen to the gospel story of Christ crucified and think nothing of it. Paul was right: Christ crucified is either notorious or glorious, but it can't be trivial. It's just too shocking.

So for the rest of this chapter, we're going to discuss crucifixion very bluntly. This is not aimed to disgust you (although it will) or to overwhelm you (although it might), but to inform you, so that the phrase "Christ crucified" can have the same impact on you as it had in the first century. If you've seen *The Passion of the Christ*, you may know much of what follows, but reflecting on it again will probably not do you any harm. After all, as we have just read, Paul preached nothing else.[1]

Crucifixion was invented by the Persians somewhere around the fifth century BC, and it continued in widespread use until banned by the Emperor Constantine in the fourth century AD. Widely acknowledged as the most despicable and disgusting way to kill someone ever devised, crucifixion has spawned its own word for intense pain (our word "excruciating" literally

---

1 It is true that neither Paul nor the Gospel writers ever described the specifics of crucifixion, except the reference to "scourging." But that is probably because crucifixion was so widely practiced that their readers already knew about them.

means "from the cross"). In essence, it brought about slow death by asphyxiation, with victims gradually suffocating to death as their lungs filled with their own fluid. It could take days to die.

The criminal was secured to the cross by means of six-inch metal spikes driven through their wrists and ankles. In itself, this would of course bring about massive blood loss, as veins and arteries were severed. The cross was then lifted vertically and rammed into a hole in the ground, at which point many bones would likely be dislocated. Hanging in the air with nothing but the nails supporting their weight, the criminal would need to push themselves up and down in order to breathe (which is why, in the gospels, the bandits' legs were broken to make them die more quickly). Understandably, to end their suffering, many victims tried to kill themselves by lowering themselves on the cross and suffocating faster, but the Romans grew wise to this and installed a seat, so that dying would take as long as possible. At each point, the objective was to make crucifixion as long and torturous as it could be. So barbaric was the process that Roman citizens and women were hardly ever crucified—and if women were, they were nailed facing the cross, so that passersby could not see their suffering. Even the Romans knew how grotesque it was.

Crucifixion itself wasn't even the whole story. Before the cross, at least in Jesus' day, victims suffered a severe penalty known as scourging, which involved being hung from a post in the courtyard while a multi-lashed whip, embedded with bone, glass or metal, was used against the back, legs and backside. A soldier would scourge in such a way as to ensure that the glass or metal got stuck in the criminal's flesh, and then rip it out, exposing the muscles and even bone. Some would die from the scourging alone, while those that survived were often, unsurprisingly, physically unable to carry a splintered wooden stake uphill afterwards. In Jesus' case, all this unthinkable pain was compounded by a facial beating with a reed, and a crown of twisted thorns. Then, while hanging on the cross, naked and with the body in shock, the victim would typically lose control of his bodily functions, adding humiliation to his pain, and he would be ridiculed and spat upon by the gathered crowd. As urine, feces, blood and sweat mingled together in a pool on the ground, the message of the cross could not be clearer: the Romans are in charge around here, and this "Messiah" is not.

All of which makes it quite staggering that within a few years, the event we've just studied had come to mean the exact opposite. According to Paul, and to thousands of people around the Mediterranean world, the events of Good Friday meant the *Messiah* is in charge round here, and the *Romans* are not. Galatians 5:11 calls this scandal "the offence of the cross." It's why people had such strong reactions to it. The Jews knew that people strung up on crosses were cursed by God, and the Gentiles knew that they were helpless criminals. So how could anyone not only admit their Messiah had been executed on a cross, but actively announce it? Put differently, how could anyone preach Christ crucified?

We need to recover our amazement at Calvary, our horror at what Jesus suffered, and our thankfulness for what he accomplished on our behalf. Most of all, we need to remind ourselves of the heart of our gospel: the proclamation of

Christ crucified. It might be idiotic or infuriating to everyone else. But to those who are called, wherever we come from, it's the power of God and the wisdom of God.

THE BLOOD OF JESUS

You were ransomed from the futile ways
 inherited from your forefathers, not
with perishable things such as silver
 or gold, but with the precious blood
of Christ, like that of a lamb without
blemish or spot.
(1 Peter 1:18–19)

How can the cross of Jesus be the gospel? How can some-thing so gruesome as the torturous death of the Messiah be worth preaching? Does such horrible violence have to be part of the gospel?

According to the New Testament, the blood of Jesus isn't one extra component of the gospel, like a shot of vanilla in a coffee, without which the gospel would be a little less good. It's like the coffee bean itself, the very heart and point of everything, without which the gospel wouldn't exist at all. The blood of Christ is essential.

We all hate blood. Some of us cope better with it than others but there's something a bit nasty about its deep red color, its smell, and its warm and sticky texture. We avoid it. We are very careful to ensure we don't see our own blood, and if we do cut ourselves, out come the Band-Aids straight away. Even though many of us eat meat regularly, most of us find the idea of physically spilling an animal's blood disgusting. We hate the consequences of blood, too: we wash our clothes if they ever get stained with it, and we shudder at scabs and hospital dramas. Blood carries life, and spilling it leads to death, so it makes us recoil, and we do what we can to get it as far away from us as possible.

That's how God feels about sin. He absolutely hates it. He recoils at sin's very sight, and despises the color, the smell and the texture of it. He hates what it is and he hates what it does to people, to communities and creation. Just as we react strongly to blood, so God reacts strongly to sin; sin leads to death, so it makes him recoil, and he does what he can to get as far away from it as possible.

There is something quite deliberate about God's decision to make blood sacrifice necessary for the forgiveness of sins. And the reason for this is not that God is a sadist or a masochist who loves blood because he loves hurting people. On the contrary, all blood sacrifices take place because he loves *saving* people. God chose shedding blood because he wanted us to feel the same way about sin as he does. He wanted us to see the link between sin, blood and death, so we could understand the consequences of our sinful behavior.

This is graphically shown in the laws about sin offerings in Leviticus 4. If a normal person in Israel sinned and wanted forgiveness, they would have to bring a goat to the priest and kill it themselves. There is nothing sanitized about this; goats would have wriggled and squealed, and blood would have gone everywhere, leaving the Israelite in no doubt that sin led to blood, and thus to death. Then the priest would dip his finger in the blood and put it on the horns of the altar (which, if you're squeamish like me, is even worse). The whole sacrifice is deeply symbolic, designed to show that just as blood seeps out of a goat when you kill it, so life seeps out of a person when you sin. Sin is serious, God hates it, and so should we. Hence the shedding of blood.

But, and this is really important, exposing the seriousness of sin is not the main point of blood. God doesn't set up blood sacrifice so we can wallow in how terrible we are, or so he can remind us of our sins. He sets it up so he can *rescue* us from our sins. In Leviticus, animals shed their blood and died so that people didn't have to; once an animal had died on behalf of your sin, you couldn't be punished for it yourself. The sin had been completely forgiven. In an even more powerful way, Jesus shed his blood and died so that we don't have to. We may feel like our sins are so heinous that we deserve death—and they are, and we do. But the gruesome consequences of our sin, the death and the blood spurting everywhere, have already happened. To Jesus.

Rebecca Pippert tells the true story of a guilt-ridden woman who couldn't believe God would forgive her. She explained, through uncontrollable tears, that she and her husband had been youth workers in a church before they married, and while going out they had started sleeping together despite the guilt she felt every time. Then, while engaged, she discovered she was pregnant. Faced with an upcoming wedding, and certain that the church wouldn't be able to cope with the shame of her pregnancy, the couple made the most awful decision of their lives. They decided to have an abortion. "My wedding day," she sobbed, "was the worst day of my entire life. Everyone in the church was smiling at me, thinking me an innocent beaming bride. But all I could think was, "You're a murderer. I know what you are and so does God. You have murdered an innocent baby." I know the Bible says that God forgives all of our sins, but I've confessed this sin a thousand times, and I still feel such shame and sorrow. How could I murder an innocent life?" At this point, Rebecca took a deep breath and said: "I don't know why you are so surprised. This isn't the first time your sin has led to death, it's the second."[1]

That's the power of the blood of Jesus. The thing you feel most guilty for—adultery, murder, pedophilia, or whatever— is actually only the second worst thing you've ever done. Because of guilt, you may feel your sin deserves some sort of violent and unpleasant response. You're right. But the violent and unpleasant response, the smell and the texture and the spattering of redness, the blood and the death, has already taken place. You are set free, "ransomed … with the precious blood of Christ."

---

1 Rebecca Manley Pippert, *Hope Has Its Reasons: The Search to Satisfy Our Deepest Longings* (Downers Grove: IVP, 2001), pp. 108-110.

THE THIRD DAY

For I delivered to you as of first
importance what I also received:
that Christ died for our sins in
accordance with the Scriptures, that
he was buried, that he was raised on
the third day in accordance with the
Scriptures, and that he appeared to
Cephas, then to the twelve.
(1 Corinthians 15:3-5)

If the gospel stories had stopped on Good Friday, Christianity
would be a tragedy. It certainly wouldn't be a gospel. If you
pause at the end of Mark 15, you're stuck with the most depressing, unjust scenario imaginable: a murderer released, the
innocent killed, black skies, terrible pain, crying women, and
a huge stone in front of the hero's tomb. At 6 p.m. on Friday
evening, all our worst fears about the world have been confirmed. Jesus fought death, and death won. If Christ has not

been raised, then Christianity is a false dawn, a rotten egg, a waste of time, and Christians are the most pitiful people on the face of the earth.

Thank God for the third day! You know the facts: a group of women go to perfume Jesus' body and find the stone moved and the tomb empty. Within a matter of hours, a number of people in several different locations see Jesus, alive and well, resurrected from the dead. This is bizarre, because not only does the pagan world know resurrection is impossible, but the Jewish world knows it cannot possibly happen like this. (Resurrection, in Jewish thought, happens to everyone at once, at the end of the age.) Announcing the resurrection seemed as ridiculous then as it does today. Yet the announcement spreads over the next few days, fuelled by the growing witness list (before long numbering at least five hundred, in a world where only two are required to establish something in court) and by the surprising failure of the authorities to produce a body. Within twenty years, news of the third day has reached Rome, and within thirty, the emperor begins burning Christians as street lights to get them to shut up about it.

Lots of modern people may not believe in the events of the third day, preferring instead some fanciful and often quite silly alternatives. But there it is anyway, the rationalist's riddle and the materialist's minefield. But why is the resurrection of Jesus a gospel story, rather than simply a set of facts? What does the third day actually mean?

If you skim through your Old Testament, you'll find the third day often carried significance. For a long time, I assumed the third day was just a statement of fact—Jesus died on day one, was in the tomb on day two and raised on day three. But there's more to it than that, because Paul says Christ was raised on the third day "in accordance with the Scriptures." When Abraham went to sacrifice Isaac, it was on the third day that God provided a substitute so that he might live (Gen. 22:4). At Mount Sinai, God appeared to the people on the third day, so powerfully that Moses had to warn people, "Be ready for the third day … whoever touches the mountain shall be put to death" (Ex. 19:11-12). Joshua (whose name in Greek would be Jesus) led the people of Israel into the Promised Land on the third day (Josh. 3). Hosea prophesied that "on the third day he will raise us up, that we may live before him." (Hos. 6:2). Substitutionary sacrifice, appearance in power, entry into the promises of God and the awakening of Israel to new life all happened on the third day.

The third day brims with meaning. It also vindicates Jesus, backing up all he taught and showing him to be in the right. If Jesus had said all he said and done all he did, but remained in the tomb, it is unlikely we'd be reading about him now, let alone worshiping him. He would have lost. It's all very well saying Yahweh will vindicate you and judge your enemies, but since you're still in a tomb, I'll take my chances, thanks. But if, after saying all these things and doing all these things, Jesus was then raised from the dead by Yahweh himself—well, that makes everything sound a lot more credible, and it might even change the world. Perhaps I'd better listen to what Jesus says about the kingdom of God after all.

Jesus' resurrection also launched God's new creation. In Jewish thinking, the resurrection happened at the end of the age, and was part of God making all things new. The third day does not mean, as often implied in songs and sermons, that

Jesus has gone to heaven and we will too, leaving the earth to its sorry fate.[1] It means that the new age has already begun, life is already overcoming death, and Jesus is the first phase of the complete renewal of everything (or, in Paul's phrase, the "firstfruits"). During the Rwandan genocide, Western countries got preoccupied with airlifting out their citizens. But really the country needed a heavyweight rescue operation to make peace, sort out the infrastructure and renew the country. God isn't like our limited governments. He's not into airlifting Christians out of the world, but is in the middle of a heavyweight rescue operation, transforming the world through them. This operation launched on the third day.

The story of the resurrection is absolutely glorious. Jesus was right, new creation has begun, sins are forgiven, death is defeated, we will be resurrected, and Satan is undone. Jesus fought death and Jesus won. The third day proves it.

---

1   This idea is tackled boldly and with clarity by N. T. Wright, *Surprised by Hope* (London: SPCK, 2007).

JESUS IS LORD

If you confess with your mouth that
Jesus is Lord and believe in your
heart that God raised him from the
dead, you will be saved.
(Romans 10:9)

Paul's letter to the Romans is an underground political
pamphlet. We tend to think of it as a theological essay, or the
original Alpha or Christianity Explored course, and in some
ways it is. But, because we don't live under the rule of the
Caesars, we probably miss the sharp political edge of the story.
Romans is dangerous, daring and dramatic, largely because of
the claim it makes about a Jew from Nazareth. If Jesus is Lord,
then Caesar can't be.

To grasp the significance of the claim, we need to get
ourselves into the Roman world of the first century. By the
start of the first millennium, the Roman Empire stretched
from Portugal to Israel, Germany to southern Egypt, and was

expanding all the time. The empire included a quarter of the world's population (and of course most in the empire had no idea that the other three-quarters existed), so it wasn't long before Rome began to see itself, and particularly its emperor, as ruler of the world. Roman citizens were required to make a declaration of allegiance to the state: "Caesar is Lord."

When the early Christians started announcing that Jesus was both risen and the Lord of the world, you can understand the danger. The disciples taught that through his resurrection from the dead, Jesus had been declared the real ruler, and Caesar was an impostor lord. The implications were clear: loyalty should be pledged to Jesus, and not to Rome. If Jesus tells you to preach, or heal, or plant churches, and Caesar tells you to shut up and stay put, you listen to the real Lord and ignore the fake one. It's high treason. It might cost you your possessions, your family or your life, but confess it with your mouth anyway: Jesus is Lord, and Caesar is not.

That's just the start, though. Paul presumably subscribed to the theory that if you're going to put the fat in the fire, you might as well throw petrol on as well. He fills his letter with sideswipes at Caesar. We know from archaeology that Roman emperors used to claim they were divine; coins were inscribed with the Latin words *divi filius*, meaning "son of the divine." Paul refers to Jesus as "the Son of God" in the very first sentence of this letter, using the exact Greek phrase used for Caesar. Roman emperors were often said to be gods after their deaths, and declared worthy of worship and obedience. Paul's political pamphlet announces that Jesus is God over all, that he alone is worthy of worship, that worshiping created beings is the essence of human sin, and that his job is to summon all the nations to obey the real Son of God.

Caesar conquered his enemies and therefore brought peace throughout the empire. The people frequently referred to him as *soter*, or "savior." Paul teaches that only by confessing the lordship of Jesus, the one who has truly brought peace by conquering your enemies, will you be saved. And this letter was written, of course, to Christians in Rome. Imagine someone pinning a copy of *The Communist Manifesto* to the Capitol Hill notice board in the 1950s, and you might get a sense of how provocative it all was.

There's more. In secular Greek, the word *euangelion*, meaning "gospel" and giving us our word "evangelize," was used in two interesting ways. Firstly, when Caesar won a battle, heralds were sent back to "proclaim the good news" (*euangelizo*). Paul, especially in Romans 10, seizes on the word to announce that Jesus, the real Lord, has won the decisive battle, and that all his disciples are now heralds bringing that news to the world.

Secondly, the birthday of the Emperor Augustus was celebrated as *euangelion*; his birthday "signaled the beginning of good news for the world."[1] Compare this to Luke's provocative announcement that brings together a whole bunch of Caesar phrases (italicized here) and applies them to Jesus:

> Fear not, for behold, *I bring you good news* of great joy that will be for *all the people*. For unto you *is born this*

1 From the Priene calendar inscription, cited in Adolf Deissmann, *Light from the Ancient East*, translated L. Strachan (London: Hodder and Stoughton, 1927), p. 366.

day in the city of David a Savior, who is Christ the Lord.
(Luke 2:10-11)

Knowing this, it's no great surprise that Paul and his companions were so often seen as political troublemakers. "These men
who have turned the world upside down have come here!"
cried the Thessalonians in Acts 17:6. "And they are all acting
against the decrees of Caesar, saying that there is another
king, Jesus." There is. That's the whole point. Jesus is Lord,
and Caesar is not.

Let me make one point of clarification here. It could sound
from all this like Caesar was the original lord, savior and son
of god, and the early Christians stole these titles to make Jesus
sound better. When you study the Old Testament, however,
you realize that these titles go back way before Caesar and his
empire, to the true Lord and Savior of whom Caesar was the
parody and Jesus the exact imprint:

Come quickly to help me, O Lord my Savior. (Psalm
38:22, NLT)

I, I am the LORD, and besides me there is no savior.
(Isaiah 43:11)

Yet I will rejoice in the LORD, I will be joyful in God my
Savior. (Habakkuk 3:18, NIV)

Jesus is Lord, and Caesar is not. Neither is the president or the
prime minister, or liberal democracy, or academic learning,
or sexual fulfillment, or tolerance, or financial gain. Those

things may be good, but ultimately they, just like Caesar, will be humbled before the throne of the one who made them, and all humanity will confess with their mouth, "Jesus is Lord!"

VIII

JUSTIFICATION BY FAITH

Therefore let it be known to you,
brethren, that through this Man is
preached to you the forgiveness of
sins; and by Him everyone who believes
is justified from all things from
which you could not be justified by
the law of Moses.
(Acts 13:38-39, NKJV)

Without justification by faith, "Jesus is Lord" might not be gospel at all. But surely the lordship of Jesus over everything is such wonderfully good news?

In sixteenth-century England, the announcement that "Elizabeth is queen" was good news to lots of people, but not for the Duke of Norfolk, or the Catholic clergy. The Normandy beach landings were celebrated by millions, but signified terrible news for the Nazis and their collaborators. More mundanely, the same weather forecast might be a source of celebration for gardeners and terror for picnickers. In the same way, the lordship of Jesus comes as bad news for people who oppose him. For everyone who collaborates with sin and rebels against their creator, which amounts to every one of us, the lordship of Jesus ought to spell disaster.

Yet it doesn't. Three words make all the difference: justification by faith. This amazing truth—that rebels and collaborators like you and me can be made right with God by faith in his Son—means the lordship of Jesus spells salvation, not disaster. Lordship without justification would be terrifying news. Justification without lordship would be trivial news. But justification and lordship combined make tremendous news.

Justification is a courtroom word. It describes the moment when the verdict is passed and the judge finds in your favor. Generally, we tend to think about justification as something that happens for defendants: a innocent man tried for murder is not sent to prison, and therefore "justified." However, justification involves not just being cleared of a crime ("acquitted"), but being vindicated—shown to have been in the right, announced righteous. In many ways justification works more like a plaintiff awarded damages than a defendant let off; more *Erin Brockovich* than *A Few Good Men*. And it happens to sinful people like you and me.

Why? How on earth can a just God look at you and me and not only let us off, but declare us righteous? One answer kicking around first-century Judaism involved God justifying people according to their faithfulness to his covenant and their obedience to the law of Moses, despite their imperfections. To Paul, however, this was appalling, since "if justification were through the law, then Christ died for no purpose." As Paul concluded in Acts 13, justification cannot happen through the law of Moses, but only through us being given the perfect obedience of Jesus, as a gift. God has both condemned our sin (in Christ), and enabled our obedience (in the Holy Spirit). Thank God for the Trinity:

> There is therefore now no condemnation for those who are in Christ Jesus ... By sending his own Son in the likeness of sinful flesh and for sin, [God] condemned sin in the flesh, in order that the righteous requirement of the law might be fulfilled in us, who walk not according to the flesh but according to the Spirit. (Romans 8:1-4)

Because our sin has been condemned in Christ, and the righteous requirement of the law fulfilled in us as we walk by the Spirit, we can conclude it is completely just of God to justify sinners. Do you see? God does not say that, because he's a nice guy, he won't condemn us or require us to fulfill the law. That would purchase our righteousness at the expense of God's righteousness. He says that because we are in Christ, *he has condemned us already*, and yet because we walk in the Spirit, *we fulfill the law*. In this mind-blowing demonstration of wisdom and teamwork from the Trinity, both sinful people (underlined below) and sinless God (italicized) are justified, vindicated, and declared to be in the right:

> [People] <u>are justified by his grace</u> as a gift, through the redemption that is in Christ Jesus, whom God put forward as a propitiation by his blood, to be received by faith. This was *to show God's righteousness*, because in his

divine forbearance he had passed over former sins. It was
to show his righteousness at the present time, so that *he might
be just* <u>and the justifier of the one who has faith in Jesus</u>.
(Romans 3:24-26)

How do we access this tremendous blessing of being declared
righteous by God?

The answer given again and again in the New Testament is
by faith. The key of faith, not circumcision or law-keeping or
any other observance, unlocks the privileges of justification,
whether you're a Jew or a Gentile. But the word "faith" can,
like "justification," be misunderstood, so we need to be careful.
There are two parts to faith, one usually far more emphasized
than the other.

Firstly, faith involves believing. This is easy to see in our
Bible translations: faith is the noun, and believing is the verb.
If you don't believe that Jesus died, rose again, and was shown
to be the Lord of the world and the Son of God in power,
then you won't become his disciple. That's why preaching is
necessary—people need to know something in their minds
before they can believe it.

Secondly, faith involves trusting. Trust doesn't simply
mean the intellectual realization that someone exists, but the
commitment of your life into their hands. When I teach this, I
often bring someone to the front and ask them if they believe
I am strong enough to catch them. They always say yes. I then
get them to close their eyes or blindfold them, and ask if they
will fall backwards into my arms. Some falter at this point, but
most give it a try. Finally, I get someone else to stand behind
them and catch them, while I move well away. With my voice

clearly coming from some distance, I then ask the poor blind-folded person once again if they believe I will keep them safe. Not many take the plunge, but the ones that do show what Paul means by "faith": they trust me with their lives, even if they cannot understand how it will all work out.

That's the sort of faith Paul is talking about. That's the way in which we receive God's gift of justification. That's the way you and I, rebels and collaborators and sinners, get made right with the Lord of the world. That's the gospel story of justification by faith.

CHRISTUS VICTOR

He disarmed the rulers and authorities
and put them to open shame, triumphing
over them in him.
(Colossians 2:15)

There's only ever been one proper victory. Literally. In all of history, there has only ever been one contest you can look back on centuries later and agree it was won, permanently and definitively, by one side. Just one. In millions of attempts.

Think about the contenders. The Assyrians beat all their rivals in the eighth century BC, but then lost to the Babylonians in the seventh, who lost to the Persians in the sixth, who got wiped out by the Greeks in the fourth, who crumbled in on themselves in the third, and so on. The Romans crushed all before them for four centuries, but they eventually lost too—just like the Goths, the Vikings, the Mongols, the Spanish, the British, and everybody since. IBM were dominant for a generation, but then lost to Microsoft, who then lost to Apple.

Empires, technology companies and sports teams seem to play a continual game of "I'm the King of the Castle." True victory—conquering all rivals completely and permanently—is unheard of.

With one exception. In AD 30, God waged a three-day campaign against all of his most powerful enemies, sometimes referred to as "rulers," "authorities," "principalities," and "powers." The main confrontation took place on a rubbish dump outside Jerusalem, where God, in his Son Jesus, met Satan, sin and death head on. A mocking enemy faced a defiant Son of God, and within six hours the one-sided battle was over and the victory triumphantly announced with the words "It is finished" (Jn. 19: 30). On the third day, the victory parade began, as the risen Champion came out of the tomb to the amazement of earth and the applause of heaven. As Paul describes it in Colossians 2:15, God obliterated his enemies in Jesus, took away their armor, and made a public spectacle of them by parading their corpses through the streets.

The Latin phrase for this—although why theologians continue to use Latin words for this sort of thing is a mystery—is *Christus Victor*, which means "Christ the winner," or if you prefer, "the Conquering Messiah." You may remember the opening battle scene of *Gladiator*, where the Romans fight the Barbarian armies of Germania. It's far from an even contest, so vast stood the might of Rome, but when the cavalry arrives the Barbarians' fate is sealed. As the camera pans round the dead bodies, a bloodied Russell Crowe raises high his sword and cries, "Roma Victor!"

The cross was such a moment, only more so, because the victory still lasts today, sixteen centuries after the collapse of

Rome. At Calvary, the stranglehold of sin was so smashed, and the dominion of death so decimated, that all those watching could do nothing but raise high their arms in triumph and cry, "Christus Victor! Christ has conquered!"

Strangely, considering how often this picture of the gospel appears in Scripture, it is not one that many of us are used to thinking about. In the West, we traditionally preach a gospel of individual forgiveness, and a cross that saves us from the wrath of God. Such an explanation of Jesus' death is, of course, completely true, but there is more to the cross than that. The cross can be described not just in terms of the lawcourt, but in terms of the battlefield. We can worship God not just for his act of compassion, but for his act of conquest. And we can focus not just on what Jesus did to us (made us right with God), but on what he did to Satan, sin and death itself (conquered them utterly). Such an understanding of the cross will not only keep us in line with the Bible, but it will also help us make sense of what Jesus is doing now. "For he must reign until he has put all his enemies under his feet" (1 Cor. 15:25).

We must be careful not to underplay the victory of Christ. Because we continue to live in a world where the rule of Jesus is not yet seen as it will be—a world where sin continues, and sickness exists, and people die—it is easy to live as if Colossians 2:15 were not true. We can slip into thinking of the cross as God's opening gambit, the means by which we will defeat Satan rather than the means by which Satan has already been defeated. By thinking like this, everything in our lives, from our evangelism to our growth in personal holiness, becomes a question of completing a victory that has not yet been achieved. The cross becomes to us as the D-day landings in 1944: the battle is not over, but the result is virtually assured, and all that remains is for us to press on until victory is complete.

That picture can be a helpful one, and I have used it myself in the past. But I think it underplays the picture of Christus Victor, Christ the winner. After all, the New Testament's theology of evangelism, let alone of sanctification, is not based on *completing* a victory but on *recognizing* one. Paul's exhortations to live holy lives in passages such as Romans 6:15-23 and Ephesians 5:7-10, are not founded on completing Christ's victory over sin, but on acknowledging it. And Peter's preaching of the gospel in Acts 2:32-36 is not about establishing Jesus' dominion over the nations, but on announcing it.

As such, the gospel of Christus Victor means that our evangelism is less like defeating the last few battalions of the Axis powers, and more like proclaiming the end of the war to the last Japanese soldiers hidden in the Philippine jungle. You may have heard about Lt. Hiroo Onoda, who refused to believe that World War II was over, and remained in hiding from 1945 until 1974, when he was finally reached by a college dropout called Norio Suzuki. He had lived under a false view of the world, pledging allegiance to a long-defeated power, for twenty-nine years. Suzuki proclaimed to him the good news that the war was over (he "preached the gospel"), and Onoda finally brought his life and his behavior in line with the truth. That proclamation of the truth—that the war is over, that the enemy is defeated, and that all people can now live in the good of the victory of Jesus—is what evangelism is all about.

Perhaps you feel the responsibility of establishing Christ's victory over darkness in the lives of your unbelieving friends. Or perhaps you struggle to believe you will ever be able to overcome the ongoing power of sin in your own life. Lift your head, and reflect for a while on Christus Victor, the only true winner in the whole of history. In other words:

> Weep no more; behold, the Lion of the tribe of Judah,
> the Root of David, has conquered. (Revelation 5:5)

THE CUP

And he withdrew from them about a stone's
throw, and knelt down and prayed, saying,
"Father, if you are willing, remove
this cup from me. Nevertheless, not my
will, but yours, be done." And there
appeared to him an angel from heaven,
strengthening him. And being in agony
he prayed more earnestly; and his sweat
became like great drops of blood falling
down to the ground.
(Luke 22:41-44)

We deserve a cup, and not in a good way. Today, the word "cup" suggests either a drink or perhaps a trophy, both very positive images. In Scripture, however, the cup often comes with an ominous note, and is the image most often used to describe the wrath of Yahweh. The fact that we deserve to drink it is bad news. Very bad news.

A quick word study will make the point. In the Old Testament, with one or two exceptions, the cup image signifies Yahweh's wrath, which those who sin against him have to drink. If we are to have any idea what Jesus was praying about in Gethsemane, then we need to understand this:

> Thus the LORD, the God of Israel, said to me: "Take from my hand this cup of the wine of wrath, and make all the nations to whom I send you drink it. They shall drink and stagger and be crazed because of the sword that I am sending among them." (Jeremiah 25:15-16)

> A cup of horror and desolation, the cup of your sister Samaria; you shall drink it and drain it out, and gnaw its shards, and tear your breasts; for I have spoken, declares the LORD GOD. (Ezekiel 23:33-34)

These graphic and violent images make us recoil by their bluntness. They communicate the sheer anger that God feels towards sin. Imagine how you would feel about a snake that had slipped into the crib and killed your baby. Sin provokes this feeling in Yahweh. We can be tempted to jump to the New Testament to make this image go away, but the wrath imagery grows even clearer there, with every single metaphorical use of "cup" referring to suffering and/or wrath.[1] By Revelation, the picture has become terrifying indeed, with phrases like "the cup of the wine of the fury of his wrath" (16:19). Scary.

---

1   The metaphorical uses of *poterion* ("cup") are: Matthew 20:22, 23; 26:39; Mark 10:38, 39; 14:36; Luke 22:42; John 18:11; Revelation 14:10; 16:19; 17:4; 18:6.

This wrath exists because of my sin and yours. It is easy to think of wrath being poured out for extreme things others do, like genocide and child abuse, but harder to see that it is also poured out for more everyday sins, like greed, lust, lying and idolatry—basically, our refusal to obey God at all times. Romans 2:5 says that it is "because of your hard and impenitent heart you are storing up wrath for yourself," which is frightening, because it means my stubborn attitude towards God causes a cup of wrath to be filled and kept in storage for the day of judgment. At some point, someone is going to have to drink it.

Imagine all the waste you had ever generated in your life was stored in a giant septic tank. Litter, Coke cans, woodchip, uneaten food, vomit, excrement—all in a huge, stench-ridden vat. Then, at the end of your life, you knew the entire tank was going to be poured over your head. That's our position with regard to the wrath of God: all our waste, our sin, our greed and our pride have been storing up God's anger. On the day of judgment, that septic vat will be poured onto our heads.

Except that it isn't. That is the wonder of what Christ accomplished. Faced with an enormous vat of God's righteous wrath due to be poured out over our heads, Jesus took our place and received the punishment instead. At Calvary, the septic tank of judgment emptied over Jesus' head instead of ours, until every last drop of sludge oozed out. The cup of God's fury was downed in One, once for all.

Hence Gethsemane. With the horror of the cross approaching, Jesus peers into the cup of wrath—physical agony combined with a spiritual separation from the fellowship of the Trinity. The perfectly holy One confronts the reality of bearing all that sin upon himself and having it condemned in his flesh (Rom. 8:3). He can see the aloneness, too. No matter how we feel, none of us is ever truly alone—we have some family or friends we can call, and relationship with God—but Jesus, abandoned and strung up, mocked by earth and forsaken by heaven, was absolutely alone. The terrible experience looming, he cries out in anguish, "Father, if you are willing, remove this cup from me," and his sweat runs like drops of blood falling to the ground. "Nevertheless," he prays in astounding obedience, "not my will, but yours, be done."

In that moment of submission, and in the hours that followed, the cup of God's anger was drained altogether for those who believe. It now stands empty. Even if as a Christian you wanted to drink it, there is nothing left; the hero of Gethsemane has cleared it completely. The massive septic tank of wrath at my pollution and slime, my sin and rebellion, has been completely poured out on Jesus, so that even if I stood under the vat myself, there would be nothing in it to fall on me. Because Jesus accepted the cup on my behalf, God's justice demands that I don't have to (1 Jn. 1:9). There is no punishment left. It has all been taken.

Next time you share the Lord's Supper, consider the cup. Remember that Jesus had to drink your cup to enable you to drink his. And do it in remembrance of him.

EVERYONE WHO CALLS

For there is no distinction between Jew
and Greek; for the same Lord is Lord of
all, bestowing his riches on all who
call on him. For "everyone who calls on
the name of the Lord will be saved."
(Romans 10:12-13)

As a child I was terrified of calling people on the phone. It was awful. I would really want to go round to a friend's house, but my parents would tell me that I could only go if I rang them myself and asked, so I wouldn't go. On one occasion, I left behind something really valuable, but because I felt too scared to phone them and ask for it back, I lost it forever. Calling can be difficult.

For me it's a pride thing, and it probably predates the telephone. This phenomenon has been around throughout history: calling on someone's name, whether by phone or in person, means making yourself vulnerable, asking them for help, and knowing that it is entirely in their power to accept or decline. Calling requires humility, an acknowledgment of need.

We find exactly that humility, that acknowledgment of need, in Scripture when people call on the name of the Lord. The earliest expression of worship to Yahweh, calling on God goes back to Genesis 4:26, and appears a number of times in the Old Testament as people ask him for things and then thank him for things. David puts it simply:

> Give ear, O LORD, to my prayer; listen to my plea for grace. In the day of my trouble I call upon you, for you answer me. (Psalm 86:6-7)

This sort of thinking sounds very easy, but is actually very humbling. For the king of Israel to admit that he can do nothing to get himself out of his trouble, but needs to call on the name of Yahweh to help him, requires an honest and unflattering view of his own abilities.

It is not surprising that Paul says those who call on the name of the Lord will be saved. We would expect that, wouldn't we? If people get saved by God they need to understand their position, believe that he is able to help, and call on him to save them—just as a man in a burning building needs to understand his position, believe that firefighters are able to help, and call on them to save him. God is loving and gracious. Whenever his people call on his name, he runs to their rescue. So far, so good.

But Paul is saying something more radical than that. He declares that *everyone* who calls on the name of the Lord, irrespective of their Jewish heritage (or lack of it), will be saved. That sort of talk puts the cat among the pigeons. It's all very well to say that God's people get saved by calling out to him for help, but to imply the Gentiles can do this too, with no descent from Abraham, no law, no land, no temple, and no history of following Yahweh whatsoever, well ... But Paul is insistent. No distinction exists between Jew and Greek. Salvation belongs to everyone who calls in faith.

Like members of the AA or the RAC in the UK or AAA in the US, the Jews belonged to a group that had certain privileges associated with membership, including the right to be rescued when they got themselves into trouble. Being members, they could call on the name of their rescuer any time, day or night, and he would come to their aid, whether in Egypt, Babylon, or on the edge of London's M25 motorway. But calling takes humility, and it takes faith. A number of Jews had stopped calling, either because they didn't realize they needed saving, or because they didn't believe God would do anything about their cry. Stranded on the edge of the M25, with smoke pouring from the head gasket, many Israelites possessed a phone and a membership card, but never called the one who could save, so they were left by the side of the motorway. As Romans 9:32 shows, being a member of the group doesn't help you if you never call in faith.

What really counts is calling to God in faith, not membership of the group. And therefore, Paul argues in a wonderful piece of God-inspired logic, *even people who are not members of the group* can get rescued if they call in faith. This happened to my wife Rachel. She broke down with a dramatic shudder on the M25, in the dark, in rush hour. Having barely reached the hard shoulder, she was in significant danger. Not a member of the AA, she had no right to call for rescue. But Rachel had read Romans 10. She knew that if she called upon the name of the AA in her day of trouble, in humility and in faith, she could become a member over the phone, and they would come to her rescue. Within half an hour, amazingly, she had joined a group she had never been part of before, received all its privileges, and been saved in her time of need. Simply by calling on their name. Just like the Gentiles.

You see, it doesn't matter whether you were born into the group. It doesn't matter whether your parents were members. In fact, there is no distinction whatsoever between members and non-members, for the same Lord is Lord of all, and pours riches on anyone who calls. All that matters is whether you call, in humility and in faith, on the name of the rescuing one. For everyone who calls on the name of the Lord will be saved.

THE END OF THE LAW

For Christ is the end of the law for
righteousness to everyone who believes.
(Romans 10:4)

Three-letter words can be deceptive. They look very simple, and you think you know what they mean, but there often turns out to be more to them than meets the eye. The English word "set," for instance, sounds very simple—most five-year-olds can tell me they've "set up the game"—yet the *Guinness World Records* informs me that set has 128 meanings as a noun and 56 as a verb. Three-letter words can sometimes be more wide-ranging than we might think.

The word "end" is like this in the Bible. At one level, its meaning is very obvious, but at another, its meaning is far richer than it first appears. The Greek word *telos*, which we translate as "end," has at least two clear meanings. It can mean simply the termination of something, as in "the end of the century." But it can also mean the purpose of something, as in "the chief end of government." When Paul described Christ as "the end of the law," he probably meant both.

Take the simplest one first. In Christ, Paul says, the law is finished. All of it. The ceremonial law no longer marks off the people of God from everyone else, because new boundary-markers, like water baptism and the Holy Spirit, have replaced the old ones (which is why the Jewish food and purity laws, not to mention circumcision, were not imposed on Gentile disciples). The sacrificial law no longer provides access to God, because Christ's sacrifice has secured forgiveness for all who trust in him. More surprisingly, the moral law no longer acts as our final authority on behavior, because we serve in the new life of the Spirit, not under the old written code (Rom. 7:6). In every way imaginable, the era of *Torah*-government is over.

The announcement that Christ is the end of the law for everyone who believes, is amazing news. It means that I am no longer under condemnation, because I have been set free from the law of sin and death. As a Gentile, it means even more than that: it means I can be part of the people of God on an equal footing with Jewish disciples. In short, the end of the law means that there may be righteousness for everyone who believes. Which includes me.

So how does this fit with Jesus' statement that not an iota or a dot will disappear from the law until heaven and earth pass away (Mt. 5:17)? If the law has finished, hasn't Jesus' prophecy been proved untrue? Not when we understand the second meaning of "end." In Christ, the law is not just finished, it is fulfilled. Christ is the purpose of the law: he is its explanation and its goal. The law, exposing sin for what it is, points forward to Jesus as the only way in which it can be kept. And because Christ fulfilled the law perfectly, those in Christ have fulfilled it as well.

I love sailing in lakes and on the open sea. But I used to hate the training sessions. The instructors would walk around you, barking instructions and making you tack, over and over again. They would drum the procedures into you: change hands, say "ready about," duck, push the rudder away from you, change sides, adjust the jib. And they would remind you that no matter how good a sailor you became, you would always need to do these things; that not an iota or a dot of their procedures would disappear until the wind stopped blowing, if you like. Because I wasn't very talented, I kept getting it wrong, and ended up either banging my head or capsizing the boat. I could not fulfill their instructions.

But my brother David could. When he and I sailed together, he took the helm, and he had the procedures down to a fine art. In fact, he was so good that I never even had to worry about them. Simply by being in his boat, I fulfilled all the instructors' commands without even thinking. I still had a responsibility to trust my brother, and not to get in the way, but I relied on his performance, not mine. David was the end of the procedures for me, not because the procedures were no longer valid, but he had fulfilled them perfectly on my behalf.

In the same way, Christ is the end of the law, not because it was inadequate but because we were. He did not come to abolish the law but to fulfill it, and in the process he demonstrated its goodness far more than we ever could have. As Spurgeon argued:

> I venture to say that if the whole human race had kept the law of God and not one of them had violated it, the law would not stand in so splendid a position of honor as it does today … God himself, incarnate, has in his life, and yet more in his death, revealed the supremacy of law; he has shown that not even love nor sovereignty can set aside justice. Who shall say a word against the law to which the Lawgiver himself submits?[1]

What a truth: Christ became the end of the law, not by ignoring it or abandoning it for being too difficult, but by submitting to it perfectly, fulfilling it, and then allowing us to fulfill it in him. The law is not only finished, it is fulfilled; Christ was not just its cessation, but its culmination, completion and climax. For Christ is the end of the law, for righteousness to everyone who believes!

---

1   Charles Spurgeon, "Christ the End of the Law," *Christ's Glorious Achievements* (Tain: Christian Focus, 2003), p. 21.

RECONCILIATION

All this is from God, who through
Christ reconciled us to himself
and gave us the ministry of
reconciliation; that is, in Christ God
was reconciling the world to himself,
not counting their trespasses against
them, and entrusting to us the message
of reconciliation.
(2 Corinthians 5:18-19)

There are two types of reconciliation in the world, and you can't have the second one without the first. The first type is vertical: peace with God. The second type is horizontal: peace with other people. And you can't have anything approaching true peace with people unless you have peace with God. I don't mean peace as the absence of war, because that gets achieved all the time, on and off. I mean Bible peace—*shalom*, wholeness, completion, welfare, safety. That sort of reconciliation with people remains impossible unless you have first been reconciled to God.

Evidence surrounds us. Stopping a war doesn't necessarily produce peace, any more than stopping an affair necessarily produces a healthy marriage. You can stop people fighting, but they will still hate one another; UN "peacekeepers" are usually nothing of the sort. You can even stop people speaking against those of other races and cultures (as happens in much of the West), but it doesn't reconcile everyone—an individual will still dislike Muslims, or asylum seekers, or middle-class people, or evangelicals. The only sure way to reconcile people to one another begins with reconciling them to God first: black and white, rich and poor, slave and free, Jew and Gentile. That is why the church is such a great idea, and why congregations filled with people of different ethnicities and races in places like Johannesburg and Jerusalem and Jackson, Mississippi witness so powerfully. It is also why fighting racism without the gospel is ultimately ineffective.

Pouring coffee on a train is achievable. Difficult, but achievable. Obviously, the steward is never quite sure if the train is going to jolt, so has to stand as stably as possible, keeping his or her eye on the cup at all times, and having a very steady hand. If the steward loses concentration, or if the train bumps on a rail, then in no time they've created an irate customer with first degree burns and coffee-stained trousers. But if the steward concentrates, and if the rails are smooth, everyone will probably be alright. Reconciling the coffee with the cup is tricky, but possible.

If the train comes off the track, however, suddenly pouring coffee becomes absolutely impossible, and very dangerous to try. The trolley, the urn and the steward are sent flying around the carriage, and everybody dives for cover; no one, steward or customer cares about the coffee order. From the second the train leaves the tracks, reconciling the coffee with the cup becomes completely unimportant. Reconciliation between the wheels and the rails surges to the top of the priority list.

We live in a world that, through our own sin and bad stewardship, has come off the rails. The world is shuddering violently, chaos where there was meant to be order, and conflict where there should be peace. In consequence, everybody on earth experiences turmoil and strife, whether racial, environmental, social or economic. All of us need desperately to be reconciled to one another. Yet this "ministry of reconciliation" will go nowhere until the world is back with God, just as the coffee will go everywhere until the carriage is back on the rails. We need peace with God even more than we need peace with each other.

What an amazing announcement, then, that "in Christ God was reconciling the world to himself, not counting their trespasses against them, and entrusting to us the message of reconciliation" (2 Cor. 5:19). In Christ, Paul says, God fixed the train back on the rails. In Christ, God brought about the *shalom* we really needed, peace with our creator, so that the message of reconciliation could be proclaimed. In Christ, God solved the peace problem at the macro-level, and now all the problems like racism, economic inequality, class war and hatred can be solved as well.

At the center of this reconciliation message stands the cross. It was the cross of Jesus Christ, where the cause of our fractured relationship was dealt with, that brought mankind and God back together again, and laid the foundation for people to be brought back together again too. Look at the sweeping language of total reconciliation Paul uses in Ephesians:

> For he himself is *our peace*, who has *made us both one* and has *broken down in his flesh the dividing wall of hostility* by abolishing the law of commandments expressed in ordinances, that he might create in himself *one new man* in place of the two, *so making peace*, and might *reconcile* us both to God in one body through the cross, thereby *killing the hostility*. And he came and preached *peace to you* who were far off and *peace to those* who were near. (Ephesians 2:14-17, my italics)

The cross means that we can be at peace with our creator, and therefore that we can be at peace with one another. And "all this is from God, who through Christ reconciled us to himself."

That's what I call reconciliation.

IMPUTED RIGHTEOUSNESS

> For what does the Scripture say? "Now
> Abraham believed God, and it was
> imputed to him as righteousness." Now
> to the person who works, the reward is
> not imputed to him according to grace,
> but according to debt. But to the
> person who does not work, but believes
> in the justifier of the ungodly, his
> faith is imputed as righteousness.
> (Romans 4:3-5, author's translation)

In 1992, Rick Hoyt completed the Boston marathon in two hours and forty minutes. There might not seem anything remarkable about that, but Rick was strangled by his umbilical cord at birth, and throughout his life was unable to control his limbs. He couldn't talk or feed himself, let alone walk, so the fact that he completed a marathon just thirty-five minutes shy of the world record is somewhat surprising. Because of

Rick's love of sport, his father pushed him, carried him and towed him for a thousand marathons and fun runs, numerous triathlons, cross-country skiing, rock climbing, and even a 3,700-mile cycle ride across the USA. Rick couldn't move. He certainly couldn't run or swim. All he brought to the table was a love for sport and a reliance on his dad. Yet he ended up completing 257 triathlons, simply by sitting there and trusting the one who was pushing him. His faith in his father meant he ended up being rewarded without doing any work whatsoever. Like Abraham.

Rather more mundanely, I tend to infuriate my wife Rachel by double-booking myself for things. I frequently forget to tell her about something I've arranged, resulting in lots of clashes, so recently she came up with a rule: if I don't write something on our calendar, I am not allowed to do it. It's a good rule, because it means it's my problem if I am disorganized rather than hers. But a while back, I had a trip away with friends that I *really* wanted to go on, yet I forgot to write it on the calendar. Disaster. All I could do was grovel and apologize, and ask her to forgive me. Fortunately, in a wonderful demonstration of grace, Rachel wrote it on the calendar for me and allowed me to go. My apology was imputed (or reckoned, or credited, or counted) to me as a calendar entry.

Abraham knows how I feel. About four thousand years ago, he believed an outrageous promise of God that he and his barren wife would have countless children who would inherit the world, and his belief, his faith, was reckoned to him as righteousness (Gen. 15:6). Note that phrase and particularly the language of accounting: because of Abraham's faith, God chose to make an entry in the "righteousness" column that "reckoned" or "imputed" him righteous even though he wasn't.[1] Remember, Abraham at the time was "ungodly" (Rom. 4:5). There was nothing in his life that made him righteous before God, but somehow, in the divine economy, Abraham's trust in Yahweh was imputed to him as righteousness.

Today, this idea of undeserved, imputed righteousness is controversial in some circles, but it really shouldn't be. For a start, the whole argument of Romans 4 is that we are counted righteous in the same way Abraham was, and Abraham's righteousness was credited to him on the basis of faith (a point Paul also makes in Galatians 3:1-9). Paul then uses a bookkeeping illustration about wages to make the point clearer. If you work for somebody, then you don't get paid out of grace, but out of debt.

Think about it. If you work hard all month, then your paycheck is not a gift from your employer, is it? But if you had done no work at all and simply trusted in somebody else's work on your behalf, then you would not deserve to be paid. Any payment you received comes as a gift, on the basis of your trust in another. Your reward, like Rick Hoyt's, would be imputed to you, if you like, through faith.

That is how you and I have righteousness imputed to us by God. We are justified when we are ungodly, not when we are good; we are justified as a free gift, not as a reward for our efforts. Our righteousness is not a hard-earned paycheck from God for all our goodness and effort. It is a gift, plain and

---

1   Both the Hebrew word *chashab* and the Greek word *logizomai* have this sense of bookkeeping, not to mention the immediate context about reckoning wages. *Logizomai* can be translated variously as "compute," "account," "reckon," "impute," "esteem" and "credit."

simple, imputed to us on the basis of faith. We bring nothing to our salvation. We simply trust that our Father is strong enough and loving enough to take us with him to victory. And because of that faith in the one who justifies the ungodly and the undeserving and the uncircumcised, we get a righteousness that is not our own imputed to us from somewhere else. For free. Just like Abraham.

> But the words "it was counted to him" were not written for [Abraham's] sake alone, but for ours also. It will be counted to us who believe in him who raised from the dead Jesus our Lord, who was delivered up for our trespasses and raised for our justification. (Romans 4:23-25)

XV

―

PENAL SUBSTITUTION

But he was pierced for our
transgressions; he was crushed for our
iniquities; upon him was the chastisement
that brought us peace, and with his
wounds we are healed. All we like sheep
have gone astray; we have turned—every
one—to his own way; and the LORD has laid
on him the iniquity of us all.
(Isaiah 53:5-6)

Big ideas are usually controversial. Galileo got in big trouble for saying that the earth went round the sun, and it was two hundred years before he was forgiven by the church. At various times in history, you would have found real disagreement over whether light travels, gravity is real and electrons exist. Move to theological concepts and the controversy heightens: the biggest debates in church history concern the most important beliefs, like the oneness of God, the divinity and humanity of

Jesus, and justification by faith. It is no great surprise that the notion of "penal substitution"—Christ taking the penalty for our sins when he died on the cross—has been so hotly debated in recent years.

A common tendency, when faced with a debate between two groups with letters after their names, is to hide under the bed and wait for the issue to pass. But this is a white flag of surrender; it means that anyone can torpedo the central beliefs of Christianity simply by writing an article questioning them. We need to engage with issues like this, and "contend for the faith that was once for all delivered to the saints" (Jude 3). Did Jesus suffer a penalty for sin (penal)? Did he die in our place (substitution)? And was God actually responsible for it all? These are huge questions. Fortunately for us, we have Isaiah 53 to help us find out.

In this one explosive chapter, Isaiah answers all three questions. Firstly, he shows us in no uncertain terms that the Messiah would suffer a penalty for sin. Look at the language of verse 5: the servant was "pierced" for transgressions, "crushed" for iniquities, "chastised" for the sake of peace, and he brought healing through his "stripes" (NKJV, a term that literally meant the black and blue bruise on wounded skin). Isaiah is not just describing a consequence of sin, but a penalty or a punishment that, somehow, corresponds to transgressions committed and a peace that is needed. So the cross is penal—the servant suffers a penalty for sin.

But secondly, the cross is also substitutionary, because of the tiny little words I missed out in the previous paragraph. Look again: wounded for *our* transgressions, crushed for *our* iniquities, by the chastisement that brought *us* peace, *we* are healed. The servant was not punished because he had committed sins, but because we had; it was us, and not him, who needed healing and peace with God. Jesus lived a sinless life, so there was no sin in him requiring punishment. If you realize that the cross is penal, then you pretty much have to believe it is a substitution as well. Isaiah certainly did.

Yet he goes further. Not only does Jesus suffer the penalty for our sin, but the sin was laid on him, and the punishment poured on him, *by Yahweh*. Modern people might twitch uncomfortably, but Isaiah could not be clearer:

> ... the LORD has laid on him the iniquity of us all. (Isaiah 53:6)

> Yet it was the will of the LORD to crush him; he has put him to grief ... (Isaiah 53:10)

We might wonder how this process works, and even what sort of God could hate sin and love people so much that he was prepared to "crush" Jesus and "put him to grief," but one thing we cannot do is pretend Isaiah 53 teaches something different. Isaiah insists upon Yahweh's commitment to one day punish the servant for the people's sins. In the shadow of Calvary, we can see what Isaiah never could—God would punish not just a faithful servant, but his own Son.

This sounds like a complete tragedy. How could any of this make Jesus "satisfied," as Isaiah puts it, or even bring Yahweh "pleasure"?

Imagine a city that insists on having a nuclear power reactor despite the protests of an environmental campaigner and his son. The city riot and threaten to kill them, calling them every name under the sun for opposing them, and eventually the campaigner and his son move thousands of miles away. Then an accident occurs. Just as the campaigner had predicted, the city faces nuclear meltdown, and thousands of lives are at risk. The only way they can be saved is for someone to enter the nuclear reactor itself and realign the power rods, but such an operation would expose the technician to a lethal dose of radiation poisoning. No one in the city volunteers.

Then, in an amazing act of grace, the father and son consider the trauma of the city and decide that the son will fly across the country, enter the nuclear reactor himself, and realign the rods, sacrificing his life to radiation poisoning. It costs the father his son, and the son his life, to rescue the very people who had rejected them. With the son vomiting and slowly choking to death, you might expect both father and son to regret their choice. But instead, deep joy runs through them both, because the sacrifice of one has brought the salvation of many. To the astonishment of all those watching the footage, as the son takes his last breath, he whispers in triumph, "Father, it is finished."

> Out of the anguish of his soul he shall see and be satisfied; by his knowledge shall the righteous one, my servant, make many to be accounted righteous, and he shall bear their iniquities. (Isaiah 53:11)

REDEMPTION

In him we have redemption through
his blood, the forgiveness of our
trespasses, according to the riches of
his grace, which he lavished upon us …
(Ephesians 1:7-8)

Some words become so religious, you forget what they mean. In the first century, "church" meant the gathering of believers in any given locality and "bearing your cross" meant walking to your death carrying the symbol of execution. As the centuries passed, though, these powerful meanings became softened: an ornate stone building or coping with a headache, respectively. When words and phrases lose their original context, they can lose their power as well.

A classic example is "redemption." Ask a random handful of Christians to explain it, and you will probably get some rather vague responses: "salvation," perhaps, or even "justification." Yet if you asked those same people to use the word "redeem" in an everyday sentence, they would know exactly what it means. They would be familiar with redeeming gift vouchers (giving something in exchange for something else) and redeeming mortgages (paying off all remaining debts). They would know that a goalkeeper who had let in a howler could redeem himself (cancel out the effects of previous mistakes) by making a superb save late in the game. They might also talk about people having redeeming features (good things which offset their weaknesses), or about finding redemption (achieving freedom and wholeness after a period of imprisonment or oppression). They might even have seen *The Shawshank Redemption*, in which the main character is set free from appalling and sub-human captivity to a life of liberty and fulfillment. They would know exactly what redemption means in everyday usage. It's just that they might never have realized that all of these things were achieved for them, by Jesus, at the cross.

They were. God gave Jesus in exchange for you and me, just like we give gift vouchers in exchange for items we want. In doing so, God canceled all debts that were outstanding against our account, in the same way as we clear our outstanding mortgages. He also canceled out the effects of all our previous mistakes and made Jesus our redeeming feature, the one who offsets and overcomes our weaknesses. Not only that, but he brought us out of imprisonment into a place of wholeness and liberty, thereby rescuing us from sin's power as well as from its punishment. If we stop and consider what "redemption" means in English, we have a huge mountain range of truth opened up to us.

For the highest peak, however, we need to think like a first-century Jew for a moment. The biblical concept of redemption comes from the Exodus: the liberation of two million Hebrew slaves from the oppression of their Egyptian masters. This act of deliverance, orchestrated by God, might be a little fuzzy in our modern minds, but to Paul and his readers the picture would have been exquisitely sharp: God's chosen people, who had been subject to crushing enslavement, abuse and infanticide for generations, set free from slavery through the most terrifying display of raw power the world has ever seen. Frequently in the Old Testament, this is the background for the word "redemption":

> I will deliver you from slavery to them, and I will *redeem* you with an outstretched arm and with great acts of judgment. (Exodus 6:6, my italics)

> ... it is because the LORD loves you and is keeping the oath that he swore to your fathers, that the LORD has brought you out with a mighty hand and *redeemed* you from the house of slavery, from the hand of Pharaoh king of Egypt. (Deuteronomy 7:8, my italics)

The Israelites experienced deliverance, but also redemption; they were brought out, but they were also bought out, ransomed from slavery by Almighty God himself.

Interestingly, in passages such as Exodus 6:6 and Deuteronomy 7:8, the emphasis is not on the transaction itself, but on the state of freedom that results from it. This is why neither Moses nor Paul make any reference to a ransom being paid "to" anyone, that is simply a misunderstanding of the metaphor. In fact, both in the Exodus and throughout Scripture, the redemption metaphor focuses on what the ransom was *from* and what it was *for*, not on whom or what it was paid *to*—it's not paid *to* anyone. God doesn't pay Pharoah for the Israelites, he frees them. When Paul talks in his letters about redemption, he makes the same point: we, like the Israelites, have been bought by God. He didn't have to pay anyone to redeem us, instead he set us free from our slavery to a hostile power—one intent on destroying us completely—and redeemed us from an endless period of imprisonment which had put our very humanity at risk. As we look behind us at the powers that held us captive, crushed beyond recognition and forced to liberate us into glorious freedom, we cannot help but marvel at the cross and at the great Redeemer who died there.

In him we have redemption through his blood, the forgiveness of our trespasses, according to the riches of his grace. Let's not forget it!

———

IN CHRIST

Blessed be the God and Father of our
Lord Jesus Christ, who has blessed
us in Christ with every spiritual
blessing in the heavenly places ...
(Ephesians 1:3)

You are currently traveling at sixty thousand miles an hour. That's about the speed of a bullet, and it would get you from London to Edinburgh in twenty-five seconds. In the time it takes you to read this chapter, you will be about five thousand miles from where you were when you started, even if you're just sitting on the sofa. You are flying through the Milky Way's outer spirals like a slingshot, being sucked around the sun by a force you cannot even imagine, and you're also turning round in a circle slowly. Even if you fixed your eyes on the wall and didn't move, in six hours' time you would be at right angles to where you are at the moment. Weirder still, you are doing absolutely nothing to cause any of these things. You're probably not even aware of them.

The earth is doing all the work. Because you are "in" it, you do everything it does, which means that you are currently traveling vast distances at breakneck speed in ways that would be totally impossible if you were "out" of it. Amazing, really.

If you think that's amazing, prepare to be re-amazed at being part of Jesus. Because you are in Christ, countless things are true of you that you have done nothing to cause, and may not even be aware of. That's the world of Ephesians 1 which lists out the most glorious catalog of blessings, each yours "in him."

Because you're in Christ, you are more blessed than you can possibly imagine. It's a simple formula, really: Jesus has been given every spiritual blessing, you are in Jesus, therefore you have been given every spiritual blessing. Flick through some of them with me.

You were chosen in Christ, before anything else existed at all: before the wheel, before the moon, God chose you—and not because you were holy and blameless, but because in Christ, God was going to *make* you holy and blameless. Your destiny became adoption through Christ, legally brought into God's family as one of Jesus' little brothers and sisters. You were blessed with glorious grace in Christ, which was gloriously inevitable, really, because being in Christ without grace would be like being on earth without gravity. You were redeemed in Christ, having been brought out of sin by his blood. You had his plan revealed to you in Christ: Jesus not only knew the plan, he *was* the plan. "In him" we have front row seats, as all things are united (you've guessed it) in Christ. You were given an inheritance in Christ, which couldn't really be larger; since Jesus is the heir of the whole world. Participating in his inheritance makes the Rockefeller children look small time. Finally, all this was confirmed in Christ with the Holy Spirit— the deposit that guarantees the transaction, the royal seal that confirms the king's handwriting, the engagement ring that promises the marriage. All in Christ.

Astonishingly, you and I contribute nothing whatever to it. We bring as much to our salvation as we do to the momentum of the earth. We couldn't choose ourselves before the foundation of the world; we weren't even there. Nor could we give ourselves a destiny, redeem ourselves, find out God's plan or wangle our way into sharing Jesus' inheritance. We could try, but we would fall flat on our face. Only in Christ are any of these blessings, let alone all of them, available.

Consider flying.[1] For thousands of years, people have seen birds soaring through the sky and some have tried it themselves, but all the attempts, from Icarus onwards, tell the same story. Our arm muscles are just not big enough, and there's a trail of corpses to prove it. If I attempted to jump off Beachy Head tomorrow and fly to France, it wouldn't matter how hard I tried, or how strenuously I had trained, I would plunge to my death just as quickly as the person who made no effort whatsoever. That's you and me outside of Christ. Complete no-hopers, and dead to boot.

Now imagine I go to Gatwick and board a Boeing 747. As I buy my ticket, I am making the admission that my own strength cannot get me to Paris, and I need to get inside something that can. So, in faith that the plane can carry me, I get on board, and immediately notice something astonishing.

---

1 I am grateful to John Groves for this illustration.

None of the passengers on the plane are flapping their arms. Quite the opposite: I see them sitting down, reading the paper, and drinking orange juice. It is almost as if they are completely secure in their *position*, and believe that they will get to Paris, and receive all the blessings of France, entirely on the basis of what they are *in*, rather than what they *do*. Which, of course, they will.

Our entire salvation is in Jesus. We have been chosen and predestined and adopted and redeemed and sealed in him. Our confidence in God's love, and our hope of sharing in the new creation, is not based in our disciplines, our families or our churches, as important as those things are. It is in Christ.

THE AVALANCHE OF GRACE

For by grace you have been saved through
faith. And this is not your own doing;
it is the gift of God, not a result of
works, so that no one may boast.
(Ephesians 2:8-9)

The grace of God is an unstoppable avalanche that sweeps all in its path. It changes the landscape so dramatically it's hard to remember what things looked like before. In Ephesians 2 alone, we find God's grace raising dead people to life, seating them with Christ in heavenly places, giving them good works to do, and uniting people who previously wouldn't have touched each other with a ten-foot pole. In twenty-two verses, the avalanche of grace changes a morgue into a temple. Watch.

The chapter starts abruptly: "and you were dead." Without passages like this, we would probably describe our rescue as gradually waking up to God and reaching out for his help, like a man at sea realizing his danger and gratefully accepting a lifeline. But Ephesians declares us far worse than that. We were dead (2:1), following Satan (2:2), and "children of wrath" (2:3). We were not drowning in our sin, we had already drowned. Cast aside the picture of a coastguard throwing us a lifeline which we might or might not grab onto, and replace it with someone walking through a graveyard raising corpses to life. "God, even when we were dead in our trespasses, made us alive together with Christ" (2:5).

By itself, that is quite an impressive avalanche of grace. You and I would be quite chuffed with raising someone from the dead. To God, however, that is just the beginning. He doesn't leave us former corpses to our own devices, but incorporates us into Christ and seats us with Christ in the heavenly places. Why? "So that in the coming ages he might show the immeasurable riches of his grace" (2:7). God showing us his grace is not just the basis for our salvation, it's the reason for it.

It might feel strange to think of ourselves "seated in heavenly places," since our bodies are still on earth. But consider a check-in queue at an airport. Last summer, Rachel and I waited in an airport queue with our economy tickets. Suddenly, a steward appeared and told us our pilot friend Rebecca had arranged for us to be transferred to Business Class. In a purely literal sense, we remained exactly where we had been before, surrounded by the same people and in the same line. But in reality, our destiny had changed, and everything was different: we started talking excitedly, and instead of dreading the seven-hour flight, we began really looking forward to it. When you and I are seated with Christ in heavenly places, our bodies stay where they are, at least for the moment, but everything else—our destiny, our desires, our behavior—is transformed completely. Because of grace.

In the meantime, God has things for us to do. God's grace shouldn't lead to inactivity; if it does, then we've misunderstood something. It is there to be shared with everyone, so that the grace of God might be seen as glorious in every country, school, hospital and office, whether in preaching or healing or integrity or kindness.

One of the most powerful workings of the avalanche of grace is to unite Gentiles with Jews in the church. In the Jerusalem temple, a stone partition stood between Jewish and Gentile areas, and a notice informed any Gentiles passing that point that they would be responsible for their own deaths.[1] Hardly a ringing welcome. Yet here is Paul, proclaiming that because of the grace of God in Christ, Gentiles could join Israel, sharing in God's promises and becoming part of his temple (redefined as his people), without any enmity, rivalry or partition. The avalanche of grace crashed down: "that he might create in himself one new man in place of the two ... thereby killing the hostility" (2:15-16).

The bringing together of Jew and Gentile in the church, to be "one new man," is stunning. It leaves no room for racism in the people of God, or for that matter sexism, ageism, or any other type of separation. Instead, the grace and wisdom of God shine out in his creation of a community comprised

---

1   John Stott, *The Message of Ephesians*, BST (Leicester: IVP, 1991), p. 92.

of old and young, black and white, male and female, Jew and Gentile, cleaner and politician; all worshiping the God of grace together.[2]

In the end, you see, God's avalanche of grace is unstoppable. Life beats death; grace trumps race; oneness defeats division; and the work of Christ turns a graveyard into a graceyard, a mortuary into a sanctuary. This is not our own doing—it is by grace, so that no one may boast. For by grace we have been saved, through faith.

---

2 It is hard to overstate Paul's campaign against racism in the early church. Ephesians, Galatians and Romans are all deeply concerned with it. "… there is neither Jew nor Greek" became something of a motto for him (see Galatians 3:28; Colossians 3:11). His home church, Antioch, was also a model of "one new man" leadership, combining black and white, Jews, Greeks and Romans (Acts 13:1-2).

—

OUR GREAT HIGH PRIEST

He holds his priesthood permanently,
  because he continues forever.
Consequently, he is able to save to
  the uttermost those who draw near
to God through him, since he always
lives to make intercession for them.
(Hebrews 7:24-25)

God set things up in Israel in such a way that you couldn't be a priest and a king at the same time. It was impossible. Priests had to come purely from the tribe of Levi, and kings had to come purely from the tribe of Judah. You couldn't do both.

With two exceptions. Firstly, the mysterious king and priest Melchizedek appears in Genesis 14 before the tribal system. His entire purpose seems to have been to point forward to the second exception, Jesus. Jesus, a king from the tribe of Judah (because of his birth), became a priest in the order of Melchizedek by the power of an indestructible life (because of his death and resurrection). Jesus combined the two key roles in a totally unexpected and seemingly impossible way: priest and king at the same time. Confused? So were the Hebrews.

If this all feels a bit technical we might wonder whether it matters. It matters enormously. Jesus needed to be a king, in order to be the Messiah. Without kingship, he couldn't be given authority over the earth, couldn't rule the nations and couldn't crush God's enemies. But he also needed to be a priest. If he wasn't, he couldn't present sacrifices to God on behalf of the people, and he certainly couldn't make them holy. If he wasn't a king, he couldn't be our Lord. But if he wasn't a priest, he couldn't be our Savior.

This explains why the writer to the Hebrews makes such a big deal out of him being both. The priests of Levi, like Aaron, had to be replaced each generation because of course they died. Jesus, the one holding the power of an indestructible life, stands to the Levitical priesthood like Mount Everest stands to a sandcastle—towering over it. He "holds his priesthood permanently, because he continues forever." And as a result, he can "save to the uttermost" in a way that the priests of Levi never could.

What did priests do? Their work involved at least four aspects, and Jesus trumps them all. Their most well-known task was to sacrifice. The priests, and no one else, could approach the tent of meeting, pass through the curtain, and make atonement for the people. We tend to remember the blood of the animal, but in the tabernacle two things were needed for a sacrifice of atonement: an animal and a priest. Here's the Hebrews bombshell: *Jesus was both*. He was the innocent sacrifice, but also the high priest who offered it. And because he was sinless, his sacrifice had the power to cleanse what the Levitical sacrifices never could: not just our sins, but our consciences as well (Heb. 9:13-14).

Next, the priests represented mankind to God and God to mankind. In Numbers 16, the judgment of God falls on Israel, and Aaron the priest has to act quickly to save them:

> So Aaron … ran into the midst of the assembly. And behold, the plague had already begun among the people. And he put on the incense and made atonement for the people. And he stood between the dead and the living, and the plague was stopped. (Numbers 16:47-48)

Human priests could fully represent mankind to God. But Jesus, fully God and fully man, can represent perfectly both ways. He can sympathize with our weaknesses, yet without condoning our sins. He is the perfect go-between. We have no need to pray to God through saints or through Mary. Jesus is the only mediator we need. He can stand between the dead and the living, and save us from God's judgment.

Thirdly, priests blessed the people. In Leviticus 9, right after the first sacrifices are presented according to the old covenant, Aaron lifts up his hand and blesses the people, showing that the offering has been accepted. Immediately, the glory of Yahweh appears and fire comes out from his presence. After making the first (and only) sacrifice of the new covenant, Jesus "led them out as far as Bethany, and lifting up his hands he blessed them" (Lk. 24:50).

Within a few days, the glory of Yahweh appeared and the fire of his presence had come to his people (Acts 2:3).

Finally, priests prayed for the people. They had to; the people were sinful, and their salvation depended on it. That's why incense burned in the tabernacle, twenty-four seven. But the priests couldn't pray the whole time. They were human, and they had plenty of other things to do. Jesus, however, faces no such time pressures. As we saw in Hebrews 7, he is able to save completely everyone who comes to God through him, because he is always interceding for them. Wherever we find ourselves right now, and whatever our plans in the next twenty-four hours, we have an advocate, our great high priest at the right hand of God, who is continually praying for us. Hallelujah!

ACT FIVE

RESTORATION & HOPE

REPENTANCE AND BAPTISM

> Now when they heard this they were cut
> to the heart, and said to Peter and
> the rest of the apostles, "Brothers,
> what shall we do?" And Peter said to
> them, "Repent and be baptized every
> one of you in the name of Jesus Christ
> for the forgiveness of your sins, and
> you will receive the gift of the
> Holy Spirit."
> (Acts 2:37-38)

So, what next? I understand the gospel, but what am I actually supposed to *do*? That's what the crowd wanted to know on the day of Pentecost too, and it was exactly the right thing to ask. Thanks to Peter, they received a very clear answer. "Repent and be baptized every one of you ... for the forgiveness of your sins, and you will receive the gift of the Holy Spirit."

Simple, really. Two things: turn your life around to follow God, and get baptized.[1] Somehow, over the generations, that very straightforward response became more complicated: get circumcised, obey Jewish food laws, do penance, say certain prayers, read your Bible, believe certain doctrines, cut your hair, stop drinking. But none of those things were in the mix originally. According to Peter on the day of Pentecost, and to Paul and the rest of the apostles, the right response to the gospel was simply repentance and baptism. That's it.

Repentance means turning around. I'm writing this gospel story in an English town called Shrewsbury, full of stunning Tudor buildings and a thoroughly incomprehensible one-way traffic system. About an hour ago, bafflement at the one-way system resulted in me driving directly towards a white van, who fortunately saw me and allowed me the time and space to *repent*—to perform a complete U-turn and get myself going in the correct direction. I followed the system round the town for five minutes, and then (to my horror) again repeated my mistake in a different place. This time, the bus driver glared at me somewhat less sympathetically, and I was forced once again into total *repentance*, this time with rather more people watching.

Repenting involves both a change of mind and a change of direction. It means driving towards God rather than

---

1 Of course, it's impossible in such a small space to be thorough in addressing the much-debated subject of baptism and there are many who take a different view to me. For a discussion of infant baptism versus believers' baptism, see Donald Bridge & David Phypers, *The Water That Divides: Two Views on Baptism Explored* (Ross-Shire, Christian Focus, 2008).

driving towards ourselves. It means agreeing that, in our time management and conversations and finances and sex lives, Jesus is Lord and we are not.

Repentance ultimately takes place in the heart and in the mind, but always results in transformed behavior. The other half of the response, however, is clearly and deliberately physical: baptism in water. Baptism is the one other thing that all believers in the New Testament do in response to the gospel. Scripture shows us that baptism is completely bound up with becoming a Christian:

> ... having been buried with him in *baptism, in which you were also raised with him* through faith in the powerful working of God, who raised him from the dead ... (Colossians 2:12, my italics)

> *Baptism*, which corresponds to this, *now saves you*, not as a removal of dirt from the body but as an appeal to God for a good conscience, through the resurrection of Jesus Christ ... (1 Peter 3:21, my italics)

We can easily fall into thinking of baptism as "just a symbol" and nothing more. But these texts place far more significance on it than that. Baptism does something. Baptism marks us out as disciples in a way that nothing else we can do does. To be baptized is to identify and ally ourselves with Jesus. It expresses our union with Christ in his death (as we go down to a watery grave) and rising (as we emerge from that grave, breathing and alive). Throughout Acts, new believers immediately got baptized, seeing the physical act of getting drenched as part of the package deal. It's quite natural that Paul and Peter's readers could look back on their conversion and baptism as one event.

At this point we can start to get uneasy. Surely baptism doesn't save you though? No, it doesn't. So, we don't have to get baptized in order to become a disciple? Well ...

To answer that, let's take a similar-sounding question: do you have to digest your food in order to have "eaten" it? Presumably, we'd all say digesting food is not the same as eating it, but it follows on pretty naturally. Of course it's possible to eat but not fully digest a meal—someone could immediately throw up or they might even die before digesting the food. But in normal circumstances, digesting follows on from eating.

The same thing is true of baptism. Getting baptized is not the same as becoming a Christian, just like digesting food isn't the same as eating it, but it follows on pretty naturally. It would be very weird to think of anyone repenting and not getting baptized, because that's what comes next: "Repent and be baptized!" Of course, in theory it's possible to repent and not get baptized, but something is very wrong if someone refuses to take that step, just like something is very wrong if we eat food but don't digest it. It suggests that their repentance might not be complete in the first place—having performed the U-turn and begun driving in God's direction, they won't want to ignore their Lord's command. So although baptism doesn't make someone a disciple, if a Christian hasn't been baptized, that needs sorting out.

How do we respond to the gospel of God? Peter's preaching is crystal clear: repent and be baptized, every one of you. It's that simple.

THE BATTLE FOR BEAUTY

And the twelve gates were twelve pearls,
each of the gates made of a single
pearl, and the street of the city was
pure gold, like transparent glass.
(Revelation 21:21)

You can usually tell a lot about someone by their reaction to beauty. Perfect in every way, God is deeply excited about beauty, and has committed himself to creating it, delighting in it and restoring it. Animals are indifferent to it; even the most intelligent monkeys don't gaze in wonder at paintings or waterfalls, and there are no post-Impressionist chipmunks or puffin poetry anthologies. Satan absolutely hates it. One of the most visible results of his deceitful stunt in Eden was that the most stunning garden in history became off-limits.

Amongst people, the appreciation of beauty can act as an indicator of maturity. Babies see paint and food as things to be played with, but young children can already use their creativity to experiment with them, and in adulthood some people spend small fortunes on gourmet meals and Renaissance art. Infants are so transfixed by novelty that they don't really register a gorgeous sunrise, but by our teens this has reversed—we can stare at the same night sky night after night and remain open-mouthed at its splendor.

However, no matter how mature or godly we are, our delight in beauty is always coupled with a sense of longing, whether we are admiring art or creation itself. It is hard to describe, but I'm sure you know what I mean: a twinge in our spirits, even an ache, that the whole world ought to be like this all the time, but it isn't. We bear the image of our creator God, and that means we have a passionate desire for beauty, both to create it and to appreciate it. When we look out upon a world so often marred by ugliness, our souls tell us it shouldn't be like that.

Our souls are right. The whole of creation is the battle-ground in an enormous fight for beauty, that has been raging since the very beginning. We humans, fickle creatures that we are, have fought on both sides in this battle, which is why we feel so confused about it sometimes. Adam and Eve were the original gamekeepers turned poachers, and we have continued their ambiguous relationship with beauty ever since: painting yet polluting, dancing yet deforesting, composing yet combusting. Even contemporary art, which often tries to shock and challenge the idea of beauty itself, demonstrates the tension. God made us for a world of sheer beauty, but the world we live in now is a battleground for it.

It hasn't always been like this. When first created, the earth sits formless and void and dark, but as soon as Yahweh starts speaking, beauty spills out all over the place, beauty that still transfixes us today—light, clouds, sea, trees, stars, fish, birds, animals. You rarely meet an artist who is completely happy with their work, but God looked at his work and "he saw that it was good" (Gen. 1). In the next scene, Genesis 2, the camera pans in a little closer so you can see the aesthetic dimension of creation more clearly, and the writer starts to inform us of otherwise pointless details like the beautiful stones found near each of the rivers (2:11-12), and the fact that the trees were "pleasant to the sight" (2:9), and even that "the gold of that land is good" (2:12). As the garden is described, it is probably the attractiveness of God's creation, rather than its moral purity or anything else, that captures our attention. In six days, God turned formlessness into ravishing beauty.

Things all change after the assault in Genesis 3. The garden is barred, creation is cursed, and the most beautiful created thing there is, God's image bearer, is corrupted. Beauty continues, of course, after the fall—the following chapters tell us of people learning to play pipes and lyres and develop architecture—but it is shrouded, as if someone had thrown a dust sheet over Michelangelo's *David*. So, Yahweh gets to work in the battle for beauty, and begins restoring the twin wonders of creation and creativity.

Most of this battle centers on the land of Israel, and the temple in Jerusalem in particular. The land flowed with milk and honey, clusters of grapes hung so large they require a pole to carry them. But before Israel even gets to the land, Yahweh prepares them for their mission to demonstrate God's beauty to the world by commissioning a tabernacle of intricate design and sumptuous embroidery. Have you ever got stuck in the back half of Exodus, and wondered why the acacia wood and fine twisted linen, the purple and the scarlet, the skilful weaving and the jewelled garments "for glory and for beauty" (Ex. 28:2) deserve describing in such detail? Yahweh intended the tabernacle to display his splendor.

This is even more true when it comes to the temple. The temple became the centerpiece of God's battle for beauty, built of endless cedar and gold and festooned with golden pomegranates. I doubt if any point in history has known such a carnival of the arts: elaborate architecture, decorated with expensive metalwork, woodwork and cloth, before which all manner of poems were composed, songs sung and dances performed, with musical instruments in abundance and the fragrance of incense throughout. Because of the beauty of Yahweh, the temple where he lived was unimaginably exquisite.

Yet it was not ultimate. For in the prophetic and apocalyptic writings, particularly those describing a new heaven and a new earth, an even greater level of beauty is seen, as the glory of God begins to fill the whole earth and not just the temple. It will even affect the animal kingdom, as lions will lie with lambs and eat straw like oxen (Is. 11:6-7). It will be the moment when the dust sheet comes back off the *David*, and the audience gasps as the sculpture now stands in full color, bright and radiant, far outstripping the original. According to Revelation 21, Jerusalem will be like a bride, perfectly adorned for her husband, gleaming like jasper, clear as crystal. This magnificent city will be perfectly cubic to please the eye, with gates of pearl, streets of glass-like gold, and foundations of a dazzling array of precious stones, filled with a light so bright it replaces the sun. None of this is functional; it is simply there to be beautiful. Like art. Beautiful, like God.

For now, we still live on the battlefield. But ultimately, imagination and creativity will triumph; and ugliness, one of Satan's chief weapons, will be banished forever. God will win, once and for all, the battle for beauty.

SANCTIFICATION

> But thanks be to God, that you who
> were once slaves of sin ... having been
> set free from sin, have become slaves
> of righteousness. I am speaking in
> human terms, because of your natural
> limitations. For just as you once
> presented your members as slaves to
> impurity and to lawlessness leading to
> more lawlessness, so now present your
> members as slaves to righteousness
> leading to sanctification.
> (Romans 6:17-19)

Be who you are. That's the New Testament approach to sanctification (growing in holiness). It doesn't matter who you
ask, increasing in godliness is simply a question of knowing
who you are, and then living that way. Peter says we've been
called out of darkness into light, so we should abstain from the

passions of the flesh. John says we're children of God, so we should live like him. Hebrews says we've been sanctified once for all, so we should pursue holiness. But the biggest champion of the idea is Paul: you've become slaves to righteousness, so act like it. That's how sanctification occurs.

His argument in Romans 6 is tremendously important, and it comes in three simple, profound steps. Firstly, you have been set free from sin. Even though Christians have been released from sin, Satan does his best to convince them they're not, and lots fall for his lie: fearful people believe they'll always be fearful, porn addicts that they'll never overcome lust, the abused that they'll never be able to forgive. So even though Christ liberates each Christian, they don't know it, so they never live that way.

A few years ago, I was driving down a lane in Devon with my cousin Seb when a young boy walked past holding a rope attached to a bull the size of a garden shed. It dwarfed our car, and was certainly many times too large for anyone to control with a piece of rope through its nose, so I was quite worried. Yet the bull seemed blissfully unaware of his power, and meekly followed the boy, which I thought very odd. I later learned, however, that farmers sometimes train bulls by attaching rope through their nose when they are very young, and tying the rope round wooden posts, so that the young bull gets used to the idea that it cannot escape. By the time it's fully grown, it's had so much experience of being enslaved by the rope that it doesn't even know it can break free. These giants can be led past my car by small children without it occurring to them to escape. Tragically, many Christians live like that. They have so much experience of being enslaved by sin that they don't even know that, in Christ, they can break free. Children of God can be bound by Satan for years without it ever occurring to them to escape.

Paul is emphatic: you have been set free from sin. That's step one. If you don't know that, then you won't grow in holiness, because you won't realize it's possible. I speak from experience here. As a teenager, I just didn't believe I could win the battle against lust, until after years of struggling someone convinced me that it was actually possible to overcome it. Freedom started from that day onwards. But step two involves the other side of the coin, and it's just as important. You have not just been released from slavery to sin, you have become a slave to righteousness. Your allegiance has not been removed, it has been transferred.

Let's say you are a British prisoner of war in Germany in 1944. Five years under Nazi command, you have spent your days repairing their machinery, building their bridges, obeying their officers and saluting their flag. Then one day the Allies arrive and liberate you. Suddenly, your ownership changes, and you become a "slave" to someone else. It would obviously be inappropriate for you to repair German guns and salute German officers now. But it would also be completely inappropriate for you to assert that, because you had been set free, you weren't going to work for the Allies either. No; you would immediately set about repairing Allied guns and bridges, and obeying Allied officers. Having been set free from serving the Nazis, you would immediately start serving the Allies.

Not only have we been set free from sin, we have become slaves to righteousness. We may occasionally serve our old master without thinking about it. But when that happens, we remind ourselves of the truth of our liberation, and we get on with serving the new master. There's no such thing as neutral, no Switzerland, in the spiritual landscape. We all fight for something. And in the case of Christians, that something is righteousness.

Step three, then, is simply the application of these two truths: "present your members as slaves to righteousness leading to sanctification." We're free from sin, we're slaves of righteousness, so we live that way. That's how we pursue holiness. We recognize who we are, we realize what has happened, and we live accordingly.

Sanctification, then, is simple. You've been set free from sin by the blood of Jesus; you've been made a slave to righteousness by the power of God; so present yourselves as the slaves to righteousness you are. Leave your old slavemaster, start fighting for the Allies, go on the charge down the Devon lanes. No longer will your actions lead to lawlessness. They'll lead to sanctification.

CITIZENSHIP IN HEAVEN

But our citizenship is in heaven, and
from it we await a Savior, the Lord
Jesus Christ, who will transform our
lowly body to be like his glorious
body, by the power that enables him
even to subject all things to himself.
(Philippians 3:20-21)

I don't know whether you've ever had crossed wires with someone, when someone misunderstands your words thinking you're saying something else. It can be hilarious at times, but it can also be very awkward. If you don't believe me, just listen in on a conversation between an American and an English person about wearing pants.

"Our citizenship is in heaven" is another example. To some, this phrase means that there's no point bothering about the world we live in now since we're ultimately bound for a place in the sky. Others react by saying that the idea of "heaven," is outdated, believed in only by those who lived before the invention of the dishwasher. Instead, we should focus on making this world better and leave heaven out of it. If the first group, as it is sometimes unkindly said, risk preaching a gospel "so heavenly minded it's of no earthly use," the second are in danger of preaching one so earthly minded it's of no heavenly use. The fact is, both groups have completely misunderstood both "heaven" and "citizenship."

The Philippians would have known exactly what citizenship was all about. Philippi was a Roman colony in modern day Greece, an outpost of the empire intended to bring Roman rule to the area. Many of the church would have been Roman citizens, some of them soldiers, and they would have been used to living as foreigners in the community, with the purpose of spreading Roman influence. If one of them was to say, "our citizenship is in Rome," it would not mean that they were other-worldly dreamers who were in Philippi for a few months and couldn't wait to get home. Nor would it mean that they had stopped believing in Rome altogether and had decided to get on with Greek life without it. It would mean that they were Roman through and through, outsiders in a strange land, but *with the purpose of making the strange land more like home*, while they waited for the emperor to come.

Which is exactly what Paul means. The church is an outpost of God's empire: a community of people whose passport is stamped "heaven" but who continue to live in a foreign land— earth—with the aim of making that foreign land more like home. We take heaven seriously, and live with different aims and different values to the people around us. We also take our citizenship seriously, so instead of hiding under the bed and waiting for rescue (or the rapture?), we live in the world with the intention of changing it. We live taking the empire, or the kingdom of God, everywhere we go while we wait for the Emperor to come.

Notice, also, the small word "our." You and I share our citizenship of heaven with lots of other people whose passports share the stamp of heaven, and that's an important part of this gospel story. Living in a foreign country feels exhausting, and sometimes discouraging, so God designed the local church: little outposts of heaven, scattered throughout the world, where we can regroup, speak our home language, and encourage and equip one another as missionaries to the world around us. Mission is hard, and these outposts prove vital for the citizens of heaven. From the earliest days of the church, Christians (and particularly Paul, who wrote Philippians) planted local churches. For citizens of heaven, they are the most empowering and refreshing places on earth.

As a citizen of the UK, I once spent a week in Nigeria on a human rights visit. I encountered lots of things that made me feel like a foreigner: forty-degree heat, monsoon rain, Islamic Sharia law, eating endless plantain, and the experience of being the only white face in the street. It was exhausting, struggling with the heat, the diet, the medicine and so on. When the trip finished, however, I had the tremendous joy of getting on board the British Airways plane to fly home. I was ushered into this comfortable reclining seat and offered a wide range of very English comforts: tea, a cooked breakfast, a copy of *The Times*. Then a voice came over the speaker, that gravelly deep voice only British Airways pilots can do: "Good morning. My name is Nigel, and I'll be your captain this morning. We're just in a queue at the moment, but shortly we'll be tootling across the runway and preparing for take-off. Thank you." There we were, on a runway in the blazing African sun, slap bang in the middle of Nigeria. Yet you couldn't have imagined a more English moment and I felt like I had already got home. It reinforced my citizenship, recharged my batteries, and refreshed my soul.

The local church functions like that—a totally heavenly place in the midst of a very earthly world, a place that reinforces our citizenship and renews our heavenly passports. But here's the thing: if you're not a missionary, church is all a bit pointless. If you're keeping your citizenship quiet, opting out of the struggle to bring heaven to earth in your office or school or family, then coming together with other citizens can seem like a waste of time. If I hadn't been abroad for a week, sitting in an aircraft cabin wouldn't have been my idea of fun. But when we're out in the world every day, bringing the empire of God into our cities, then local churches like Philippi—functioning as army barracks, not social clubs—are just what we need. So as citizens, let's bring heaven to earth as we wait for the Emperor to come back:

> Let your kingdom come near! Let your purpose come about, over the earth in the same way as in heaven! (Matthew 6:10, author's translation)

V
—

CREATION SET FREE

> For the creation waits with eager
> longing for the revealing of the
> sons of God. For the creation was
> subjected to futility, not willingly,
> but because of him who subjected
> it, in hope that the creation itself
> will be set free from its bondage to
> corruption and obtain the freedom of
> the glory of the children of God.
> (Romans 8:19-21)

Think for a moment about the most spectacular place you have ever seen. It could be somewhere you've actually visited, or it could be somewhere in a holiday brochure. My personal choice is the New Zealand South Island, where the mountains are so crisp and the valleys so sweeping you almost wish *The Lord of the Rings* had binned the hobbits and filmed the scenery for nine hours instead. Yet all of the spectacular sights you pictured, and many more besides—shooting stars, Alpine glaciers, African dawns, thunderstorms—have one thing in common. They all lie under a curse of fruitlessness.

It was Adam's fault. He governed creation poorly, and as a result Yahweh cursed the ground, saying it would produce thorns and thistles. The abundance and fruitfulness originally created in the garden was lost, and replaced by a world with weeds and stinging nettles and mosquitoes and famine. The curse on creation, just like the curses on man and woman, was God's righteous and inevitable response to the fall.

However, just like the curses on man and woman, God intended the curse on creation to be temporary. Not because he would eventually forget his curse (the serpent, in fact, will remain under it forever), but because he would eventually overcome it. This is the point of the well-known announcement that in the new creation, "no longer will there be anything accursed" (Rev. 22:3). Likewise, Paul makes the point in Romans 8 that creation was subjected to futility and decay, but with the wonderful hope that it would one day "obtain the freedom of the glory of the children of God." So creation groans under a curse, but only for now. The incorruptible life of Jesus is breaking out everywhere, so much so that eventually the earth itself will be released from its fruitlessness and set free to become all it was originally designed to be.

This opens up some staggering possibilities. When I consider the Amazon jungle, where every acre has around three hundred species of trees plus three hundred types of other plants, I am given to wonder: if the earth teems with life under a curse of fruitlessness, what will it look like when the curse is removed? If the Grand Tetons and the Serengeti Plain and the Californian Redwoods and the Maldives are subjected to futility for the moment, then what can we expect when Jesus returns to make all things new? Planet earth, no doubt, will be liberated into levels of wonder and glory currently only hinted at. Who knows what outbreaks of life and fruitfulness we'll see in the universe! We can be certain that the glory of the renewed creation will dramatically outstrip the present one.

This correspondence between failure and futility, or between righteousness and restoration, runs throughout Scripture. The first sin resulted in fruitlessness, and the combined sins of humanity in Noah's day led to much of creation being destroyed. On the other hand, Yahweh's promise of a land flowing with milk and honey signaled his favor to his people, and he instructed them in the clear correlation between their obedience and their harvests, and even the weather (Lev. 26:3-4). Ever since, the faithfulness of mankind and the fruitfulness of earth have corresponded to one another. The prophets were so excited about the restoration of God's people, and about the effect this would have on creation, that they couldn't contain themselves, using quite bizarre images to convey the latter: mountains overflowing with wine (Amos 9:11-15), hills singing and trees clapping their hands (Is. 55:12-13) and so on. Paul's announcement that the restoration of humanity would lead to the restoration of creation itself should not come as a surprise. The whole of history has been pointing to it.

Ultimately, although this glorious hope motivates our obedience, and although we can dream and speculate, it is impossible to fathom what creation set free will look like. We have hints in the Bible, but that is all. When all is said and done, we are trying to imagine the unimaginable. C. S. Lewis put it like this:

> You may have been in a room in which there was a window that looked out on a lovely bay of the sea or a green valley that wound away among mountains. And in the wall of that room opposite to the window there may have been a looking glass … And the sea in the mirror, or the valley in the mirror, were in one sense just the same as the real ones: yet at the same time they were somehow different—deeper, more wonderful, more like places in a story: in a story you have never heard but very much want to know. The difference between the old Narnia and the new Narnia was like that. The new one was a deeper country: every rock and flower and blade of grass looked as if it meant more. I can't describe it any better than that: if ever you get there you will know what I mean. It was the unicorn who summed up what everyone was feeling. He stamped his right fore-hoof on the ground and neighed, and then cried: "I have come home at last! This is my real country! I belong here. This is the land I have been looking for all my life, though I never knew it till now. The reason why we loved the old Narnia is that it sometimes looked a little like this."[1]

No wonder creation waits "in eager longing." Do you?

---

1   C. S. Lewis, *The Last Battle* (New York: Macmillan, 1970), p. 171.

vi

MEANING REINSTATED

So I hated life, because what is done
under the sun was grievous to me, for
all is vanity and a striving after wind.
(Ecclesiastes 2:17)

On March 1, 1942, my grandfather's ship was sunk in the Java Sea. He was captured by the Japanese and taken to a prisoner of war camp in Kyushu, where he spent the next three years before being moved to Manchuria. He didn't talk about it much. Most people who have experienced similarly traumatic events will know why. But one detail I remember him mentioning was how he and his fellow inmates put a curiously high value on knitting needles. When I first heard that, I assumed it was because they could help you escape (although how exactly that would work, I never figured out). But no—it was because life in the camp was so repetitive and meaningless that the only thing to do with the time was to unknit your clothes and then knit them back together again. Imprisonment, physical abuse and near starvation are terrible ordeals, but you can survive them if you have something to live for.

You and I are not supposed to live in futility. It kills people. God designed us to live with meaning, with intention. The first thing God ever gave Adam, before animals or commandments or a wife or even clothes, was a job (Gen. 2:15). In a perfect world, with no sickness to cure and no dishes to wash up, God gave man a job to do. Why? Because God created us to function best when we have things to do, things which matter, things which have a purpose that honors God and benefits people. It's in our DNA. Meaninglessness stinks.

It always has. That's why the writer of Ecclesiastes, at least at this point in the story, hates life. People can act as if they're very cutting edge and original for saying things like "I hate life" on albums or T-shirts, but in doing so they just prove the writer's other point—that "there is nothing new under the sun." Pointlessness always leads to despair.

Not only is the statement "all is vanity" not new, it also isn't true. Far from it. Sure, a lucky dip approach to Ecclesiastes could give you that impression, but reading the whole thing, it becomes clear "all is vanity" only in a life *without God*. Getting rich is vanity, the writer of Ecclesiastes argues; the obituaries in *Forbes* seem to bear that out. Having sex with lots of people is a striving after the wind, he says; just ask a celebrity five years after you last saw her in *Hello* magazine. But that doesn't mean that you cannot find meaning. It simply means that you cannot find meaning in the places people usually look for it: wealth, sex, knowledge, power, whatever. If everything "under the sun" is meaningless, then maybe we had better look for meaning somewhere else.

That's where Jesus comes in. Never in human history has anyone lived with such a clear sense of destiny and purpose. Prophesied over before birth, and with a clear understanding of his calling by the age of twelve, Jesus lived like a man on a mission from childhood to resurrection, and brushed aside obstacles so firmly he made Winston Churchill look like a ditherer: "Get behind me, Satan!" (Mt. 16:23). "Whoever is not with me is against me" (Lk. 11:23). "Go and tell that fox … I cast out demons and perform cures today and tomorrow, and the third day I finish my course" (Lk. 13:32). "Leave the dead to bury their own dead. But as for you, go and proclaim the kingdom of God" (Lk. 9:60). We might think this sort of lifestyle direct, or even abrupt, but the one thing you cannot call it is meaningless; the kingdom of God was at hand, and futility and pointlessness had no place there. While Jesus was inspiring to some, challenging to others and infuriating to many, he was boring to no one. Life was too short.

And so began the reinstatement of meaning—not just in Jesus' own life, but in the lives of virtually everybody he touched. Jesus brought, and still brings, an uncountable number of people into his mission to proclaim the kingdom of God. Look at what happened. Deadbeat fishermen became apostles. Tax collectors wrote books that are still bestsellers today. Once-broken, demonized women became the first witnesses of the new creation. Arrogant thugs turned into church planters.

By the sheer purpose with which he lived, the man of meaning had taken on futility and won, leaving its wreckage strewn throughout first-century Palestine and giving purpose to generations ever since. Simply by joining him on his mission, millions of middle managers and elderly ladies and self-harming students and disillusioned husbands have had meaning reinstated. They, and we, have gained the enormous privilege of knowing the big picture behind God's Word and God's world, what Paul called the "plan for the fullness of time, to unite all things in [Christ], things in heaven and things on earth" (Eph. 1:10). Even when work, family, church or whatever seems a bit pedestrian, there is still a job to do, a kingdom to build for, a world to heal and a gospel to share.

So don't listen to Marcel Duchamp, or Jean-Paul Sartre, or whoever else might be telling you that everything is pointless. Because of Jesus, and the kingdom project he kickstarted, futility is very, very last season. Meaning is back.

vii

—

THE RESURRECTION FROM THE DEAD

For as in Adam all die, so also in
Christ shall all be made alive.
(1 Corinthians 15:22)

Some of the most profound gospel stories in Scripture can be the most baffling. I don't know why; maybe God made them difficult so we'd have to think about them more carefully. Lots of the big ideas in Christianity are extremely hard to understand—the Trinity, predestination, Jesus as fully man and fully God, and so on. But one that gets less attention than most, despite being very important and very confusing, is the idea that both our death and resurrection take place because we are "in" someone else. If we don't really get this story, then we wobble through life without any real certainty of our future. If we do, however, it's dynamite.

Look again for a moment at 1 Corinthians 15:22: "as in Adam all die, so also in Christ shall all be made alive." This is the sort of sentence we can often just skim over without realizing what it's saying, so we need to slow down a minute. Paul teaches that we die because we are "in Adam," and that in the same way, we will be made alive because we are "in Christ." Both here, and in more detail in Romans 5, Paul explains that we do not die because we sin—we die because we are in Adam. And in exactly the same way, we do not get made alive because we are righteous. We get made alive because we are in Christ.

For people in Western, capitalist, individualistic countries, this seems bizarre in the extreme. It sounds like the definition of unfair. Try as we might, most of us cannot understand how we could ever be treated in a certain way because we are "in" someone else; our whole society is built on the basis that you are rewarded or punished because of your behavior, not someone else's. When it comes to the resurrection, many disciples struggle to be certain that they will be raised from the dead, to an unimaginably glorious and wonderful future with Jesus in the new heavens and new earth, simply because they are in Christ. Therefore many live without an eternal perspective, deciding instead to pursue things that this world has to offer, a bit like an engaged young man sleeping with his ex-girlfriend in case the wedding to his fiancée doesn't work out. Uncertainty leads to ungodliness.

Yet certainty is exactly what Paul has when it comes to the resurrection, because he understands what it is to be "in Adam" and "in Christ." We tend to see the human race individualistically, and reckon dying because of Adam's sin is like getting grounded because our older brother crashed the car. But Paul sees the human race organically, and reckons that it is perfectly reasonable (and deeply wonderful) for God to treat us as part of a connected whole.

Let me illustrate. If I were to be stabbed in the chest, it would make no difference whatsoever to the wellbeing of my next-door neighbor, because we are separate and distinct beings. My stab wound would not result in him being short of breath, or spluttering, or collapsing. But my being stabbed in the chest would make an enormous difference to the wellbeing of my kidneys, and my brain, and my left eye. Within a few minutes of being stabbed, my kidneys would stop filtering, my brain would stop processing, and my left eye would stop seeing. Human beings are an organic whole, so what happens to one affects all the others.

It would obviously be completely ridiculous for a cellular biologist to look at me afterwards and say, "How unfair! His left eye didn't get stabbed, yet it died anyway, despite not sharing a single cell with the heart. Only the heart got stabbed, so only the heart should perish." We all know that the body is a whole. The left eye didn't die because it did anything wrong; it died because it was inseparably connected to the rest of me. It died because it was "in Andrew." That is how the Bible views humanity. "In Adam" means what happened to him happened to us.

But now imagine a first aider arrived and resuscitated me with a defibrillator, bringing my heartbeat back to a normal rhythm and supplying oxygen to the rest of my body. My kidney would start filtering, and my brain would start processing, and my left eye would start seeing. Again, our biologist might look at my eye and wonder why it could see, since the defibrillator went nowhere near my face. But of course the eye would not be able to see because it had done anything—it would only be able to see because it was part of a larger organic whole in which life had overcome death. "In Andrew, all the body has been made alive."

That's where you and I stand in connection with Christ. We will be raised because we are in him, and he has overcome death in himself. There is no doubt here, you see; someone in Christ cannot fail to be resurrected from the dead, any more than one of my organs could remain dead while it was part of a living person. What happened to him will happen to us.

That certainty of resurrection is immensely powerful. As long as Jesus' tomb remains empty—and it's been empty for two thousand years—we can have absolute confidence that life has overcome death for anyone who is in Christ. We can be certain that we will be given new bodies when he returns, life *after* "life after death," to inherit the new creation where no suffering or sin or sickness or separation survives. People who know this live radically. Sure of their resurrection in Christ, they give their time and their finances and their lives for the coming age, and they do so with joy, happily lumping poverty and hardship in the present if it will lead to a more glorious resurrection. They store up treasures in heaven, run in such a way as to get the prize, and suffer with joy because they know what's coming. This is Paul's conclusion after his chapter on resurrection. Listen:

> Therefore, my beloved brothers, be steadfast, immovable, always abounding in the work of the Lord, knowing that in the Lord your labour is not in vain. (1 Corinthians 15:58)

THE FALL OF BABYLON

After this I saw another angel coming down
from heaven, having great authority, and
the earth was made bright with his glory.
And he called out with a mighty voice,
"Fallen, fallen is Babylon the great!"
(Revelation 18:1-2)

The Bible is a tale of two cities. There is Jerusalem: God's city, the city of peace, the joy of the whole earth, the home of God's people. But there is another city, a darker city, that runs alongside throughout the whole story. This is mankind's city, the city of war and lust and anger and jealousy, of greed, lies, prostitution, violence and injustice. She wages out and out war to destroy the city of God, from her foundation in Genesis 10 to her destruction in Revelation 18, and she hates God's people and everything they stand for. Her name is Babylon.

She is a master of disguise. Although in her earliest days she took the form of a physical city—the city of Babel, founded by Nimrod and home of the infamously smug "tower with its top in the heavens" (Gen. 11:4)—she has continually changed shape, kept up with the times, and wormed her way into every human culture. In the seventh century BC, the geographical city of Babylon was Israel's chief enemy, and ended up taking God's nation into exile in three phases, before destroying Jerusalem and the temple altogether. But when God sent the Persians to wipe out Babylon, she morphed, like a shape-shifter, into something else. Her bricks and mortar were destroyed, but her spirit lived on. In ancient Rome, she fostered lustful, brutal, God-hating paganism, an ugly force contending with the early church. Ever since, she has stayed sharp, always seducing, always evolving, always catering to whatever sinful desire is in fashion: greed in New York, sex tourism in Phnom Penh, organized crime in Moscow, religious oppression in Mecca, whatever it takes to suck people away from the living God. She loves it.

She loves all forms of idolatry. When people give their lives to money, sex or power, she is delighted. She had a ball when the French revolutionaries turned Notre Dame into a "temple of reason," and when Wall Street bankers jumped out of windows because they had lost money, and when Nietzsche said that God was dead and humility was a sickness, and when philosophy students read him and fell for it. She rejoices when human beings behave as if they do not bear the image of God, which means she is a particular fan of casual sex, self-harm, human trafficking, abortion and racism. If anything destroys the dignity of people and the worship of God, she will do whatever she can to promote it.

Lined up against her is the city of God, Jerusalem. Like Babylon, she also began as a physical place, but she soon became used as a symbol for all God's people.[1] Like Babylon, Jerusalem

---

1 See for example Galatians 4:26; Hebrews 12:22-24; Revelation 21:2-3.

has managed to affect human cultures all around the world—in contrast to all other religions, which are still centered on their place of origin (the Middle East for Islam, India for Hinduism, China for Buddhism, Europe for secularism). Jerusalem has flourished in Israel, Turkey, Rome, Northern Europe and North America, and is now more influential in Asia and Africa than anywhere else. Like Babylon, she is a spiritual city existing since time began. Yet in all other ways, she is the absolute opposite. Where Babylon celebrates idolatry and immorality, Jerusalem is filled with peace, beauty, justice and the worship of God. No wonder the psalmist calls her the joy of the whole earth (Ps. 48:2).

With opposites like this, you would expect the battle between them to be ferocious. Well, it is and it isn't. Babylon stands hell-bent on the total destruction of Jerusalem, that's for sure. She hates God, hates justice, hates Christians, and is out to kill them all. Revelation 17:6 describes her as "drunk with the blood of the saints." But Jerusalem does not respond in kind. She doesn't fight with swords or missiles or suicide bombs, but with service, building a local church (a little Jerusalem) within each and every expression of Babylon, a city within the city. A city that loves and serves and preaches the gospel. That's why the early Christians, faced with Babylon dressed as Ephesus and Corinth and particularly Rome, formed local churches instead of armies. They knew that the way to defeat Babylon was not by running away from her, nor by shutting themselves in behind their city walls and throwing things at her. It was by burrowing into her as deeply as possible, through love and service, and destroying her idolatry *from the inside*.

In the movie *Armageddon*, a meteor the size of Texas is set to hit the earth and wipe out everybody. As NASA meet to work out how to destroy it, an army general suggests firing nuclear weapons at the meteor. The head of research responds that this is a terrible idea—the meteor is just too big for that. Instead, he argues, they need to land on the meteor, drill down into it as deep as possible, and then set off a bomb. Because of its new position in the heart of the asteroid, the entire thing will explode into pieces. The meteor can only be destroyed from within.

That's how Jerusalem destroys Babylon. It's not the church's job to fire her nuclear weapons at Babylon, hoping to out-muscle or out-fight her. Sadly, this is how some Christians think, but it's far from the approach Jesus used. Instead, it's the church's job to get as deep within Babylon as possible, understanding her culture in order to love and serve people in every city in the world, and liberating others from the evil that oppresses them. That's what William Wilberforce and Martin Luther King and Jackie Pullinger did. That's what Jesus did. That's how the church of God fights, and despite her power, Babylon has no reply to it. She never has, and she never will.

Which is why she is doomed to fall. And so, when Jesus returns, we will see the utter destruction of sick, twisted Babylon and everything she stands for—all her greed, injustice, lust, pride, self-harm, genocide, hatred and idolatry. On that day, evil will be obliterated once and for all, and the noise of celebration will be overwhelming:

> "Hallelujah! Salvation and glory and power belong to our God, for his judgments are true and just; for he has judged the great prostitute who corrupted the earth with her immorality, and has avenged on her the blood of his servants." Once more they cried out, "Hallelujah! The smoke from her goes up forever and ever." (Revelation 19:1-3)

THE LAST ENEMY

But each in his own order: Christ the
firstfruits, then at his coming those
who belong to Christ. Then comes the
end, when he delivers the kingdom to
God the Father after destroying every
rule and every authority and power.
For he must reign until he has put all
his enemies under his feet. The last
enemy to be destroyed is death.
(1 Corinthians 15:23-26)

Most thrillers follow the same format. There is a hero, a
problem to be solved, someone to be rescued against impossible odds (usually a lover or a child), and a bunch of enemies to
be destroyed. Usually there are ups and downs, and if the story
is well-told there will be moments when all genuinely appears
hopeless, but one by one the hero overcomes the enemies,
until just one remains: the big one, the criminal mastermind,

the last enemy. This villain usually gets destroyed at the very end; it wouldn't really be the same if Alan Rickman died half way through *Die Hard*, or if Jack Bauer killed the chief terrorist by eleven o'clock in the morning. The last enemy gets killed at the end because he is the hardest to destroy, and the reason all the other enemies are there.

Many gospel stories follow the thriller format very closely. Jesus is the hero, the problem is human sinfulness, the people of God are in need of rescue against impossible odds (and wonderfully are portrayed both as Jesus' bride and God's child), and there are a bunch of enemies to be destroyed. Temptation is resisted. Sickness is sent packing in all its forms. Sin itself does not even get a look in. Demons are dismissed with extreme ease: "Be silent, and come out of him!" (Mk. 1:25). Even boisterous storms are told to shut up. As Jesus approaches Jerusalem, and the chief villain, we can look back over a three-year thriller in which all other enemies have been outmanoeuvred and overpowered by Israel's hero. We are now ready for the final showdown with the last enemy.

That last enemy, the ultimate villain, is death. It first entered the story back in Genesis 3, and since then it boasts a one hundred percent record, crushing all comers. The best and the brightest, the swiftest and the strongest—not one managed to defeat death. There has never been a fall in the death rate, no matter what statistics tell you; Penicillin and heart surgery and chemotherapy, as wonderful as they are, merely postpone the inevitable.

Which all makes Jesus pretty extraordinary. Of course, he tackled all of death's stooges, if we can call them that, in his earthly ministry. He fought disease by healing people left, right and center. He fought famine by feeding the multitudes, war by teaching people non-violence, demons by casting them out, and injustice by standing up for the poor and the widow. He described his work as the fulfillment of Isaiah 61, battling against poverty and captivity and bondage and oppression. He then gave his followers the same mandate. But the masterpiece of his ministry was the final showdown with death. By dying and rising again, Jesus took the worst death could throw at him and still came up smiling. On Easter Sunday, the dominion of death was broken.

So why do people still die? Surely, if Jesus fought death and won, we should jump straight into the new heavens and new earth, complete with new bodies, a sin-free world and the destruction of death altogether? That confused the Corinthians. They were puzzled that the resurrection was occurring in two stages—Christ, then everyone else—and wondered if that meant Jesus hadn't really risen after all. Paul explained it carefully.

Firstly, he said, you have to understand that Jesus was the firstfruits of the resurrection, the early crop that guaranteed the rest was coming. Paul says we are living in between the two. It's like waiting for the harvest when the firstfruits have come through, or like waiting for the thunderclap when you've seen the flash of lightning. You know that lightning will result in thunder, and firstfruits in a crop, but until it does you have to wait. It's the same with resurrection: Jesus' defeat of the last enemy means we will definitely be raised, but we're currently still waiting.

Secondly, Paul argued, death was deliberately being destroyed last so that the kingdom of God could gradually be established over everything: "he must reign until he has put all his enemies under his feet." Death, by divine design, is destroyed at the end, because it is the chief enemy. Jesus could quite easily have abolished death altogether on Easter Sunday, and brought about the new resurrection body immediately. But he wanted to establish his kingdom through people, to fill the earth with disciples, and use those disciples to demonstrate his lordship over sickness and famine and war and demons and injustice. He also wanted the maximum number of people to repent and be rescued—so, while people certainly continue to die, they also continue first to live with opportunities to hear the gospel. Therefore Jesus waited until the latest possible moment, the last trumpet, before destroying death and handing over the kingdom to his Father. Peter made the same point:

> The Lord is not slow to fulfill his promise as some count slowness, but is patient toward you, not wishing that any should perish, but that all should reach repentance. (2 Peter 3:9)

In the meantime, there is work to be done, to see God's kingdom come over every rule, authority and power. Death has been dealt a death blow, but is still causing trouble, like a man falling from a skyscraper trying to take as many people down with him as he can. So we have prayers to pray, jobs to do, injustices to fight, sicknesses to heal, demons to cast out, and a gospel to preach, while we wait for the rest of the harvest, the thunderclap, the last enemy to be destroyed. That's for starters, anyway…

X

THE WEDDING

> Hallelujah! For the Lord our God the Almighty reigns. Let us rejoice and exult and give him the glory, for the marriage of the Lamb has come, and his Bride has made herself ready.
> (Revelation 19:6-7)

We all live happily ever after. That's how the story ends. Scripture tells us a stormy tale of a complicated relationship, with more ups and downs than a child on a trampoline, but it all ends well. In the glorious closing chapters of Revelation, the story reaches its magnificent climax. The biggest wedding you'll ever see.

It didn't look like we'd get a happy ending, though. For much of the Bible, the relationship between God and his people looked like it would instead end tragically with a messy divorce, not a white wedding. It's a depressingly repetitive story at times: Israel runs off with other gods, God judges her, Israel repents, God forgives, Israel runs off with other gods ...

Because of this cycle, the prophets use very strong and sometimes shocking language. They speak of Israel as an adulteress, a prostitute, a cheap whore. Listen:

> How the faithful city has become a whore, she who was full of justice! (Isaiah 1:21)

> You have played the whore with many lovers ... You have polluted the land with your vile whoredom. (Jeremiah 3:1-2)

> And your renown went forth among the nations because of your beauty ... But you trusted in your beauty and played the whore because of your renown and lavished your whorings on any passerby. (Ezekiel 16:14-15)

> They sacrifice on the tops of the mountains and burn offerings on the hills, under oak, poplar, and terebinth, because their shade is good. Therefore your daughters play the whore, and your brides commit adultery. (Hosea 4:13)

The last of these quotations is taken from one of the few men in history who has known how God feels. God commissioned the prophet Hosea to marry a prostitute, so that he might understand what it was like to experience persistent sexual immorality. It's a horrible and disturbing idea, and it's meant to be, because it shows how Israel acted towards God. Continually, deliberately unfaithful.

There was a second reason why God told Hosea to marry a prostitute. He wanted to show Hosea how great his love was for Israel, in spite of her unfaithfulness. In passages charged with emotion, God explains that, although Israel's immorality is appalling, his love is so great that he will remain committed to her. Let's be clear: this is not a statement that Yahweh is prepared to work on the relationship, as if it could go either way. Although the immorality is entirely Israel's fault, God's love for her is so overwhelming that he simply cannot abandon her.

It is this unconquerable, incomparable love that makes restoration possible. A child's bedroom wall may be stained with ugly crimson scribbles, but no crayon can withstand repeated coats of paint. And the restoration is completely one-sided. In most romantic comedies, the happy ending is reached by effort on both sides, but not in Scripture. The romance between God and his people is restored by God alone, in Christ alone, through the cross alone. At the cross, in fact, the ceaseless love of God transforms his people altogether, from dirty whores to spotless brides, from graffitied walls to gleaming new paint, in the most movingly romantic action any husband has ever taken:

> Christ loved the church and gave himself up for her, that he might sanctify her, having cleansed her by the washing of water with the word, so that he might present the church to himself in splendor, without spot or wrinkle or any such thing, that she might be holy and without blemish. (Ephesians 5:25-27)

Can you believe that? We don't come to our senses and clean ourselves up, and God doesn't ignore our filth and decide he can live with it. Instead, he acknowledges our impurity, and then obliterates it. Utterly. He takes all our adultery and whoredom upon himself, remaining faithful even when we are faithless, and clothes us in the purest, whitest garments imaginable. He turns our cheap perfume and tacky miniskirt into a stunning, dazzling wedding dress. He styles our hair and adds the perfect accessories. He makes our bloodshot eyes sparkle with delight, and our knife-slashed forearms smooth and free from scars. And then, with tears of joy in his eyes as he gazes on the bride his own love has made beautiful, he takes the largest megaphone he can find and says to the world: "Look! My church, the belle of the ball! The most beautiful woman in the world. The bride of Christ."

Jesus is coming back for a wedding. It will be a wedding that makes all our attempts at celebration look half-baked in comparison. The feast will never stop, the wine will never run dry and the dancing will never end. You and I, if we're part of the church of God, will be there—not as a guest, or even an usher, but as the bride herself, the one who cuts the cake and appears in all the photos. Invite all your friends. The wedding approaches.

FACE TO FACE

For now we see through a glass,
darkly: but then face to face.
(1 Corinthians 13:12, KJV)

My wife Rachel gave me permission to tell the story of when she accidentally went to the bathroom in front of a whole bunch of people at a dinner party. We were at a friend's house for dinner with a number of others, all of whom we knew, but none very well. Just before dinner, Rachel went to the bathroom at the end of the corridor. She did what all of us would have done: she walked in, shut the door and bolted it, and sat down. She noticed nothing unusual. She then saw the rest of the dinner party wandering along the corridor towards the kitchen. Again, nothing. Then suddenly, the thought occurred to her: why can I see those people? How could that be possible? It then hit her like a punch in the stomach. *If I can see them, then they can see me.* For some reason, our friends had used clear glass on their toilet door, with a blind that was sometimes up and sometimes down. On this occasion, it was up. You can imagine her panic. Our friend saw what was happening and leaped to her aid, blocking the door so that no one else could see her. But it was too late. A dinner party had seen Rachel going to the toilet, and the result was extreme embarrassment (for her) and extreme laughter (for everyone else). She had assumed she was looking "through a glass, darkly," but was actually visible "face to face."

When Paul wrote 1 Corinthians, he was not talking about frosted glass on toilet doors. He was probably referring to the polished bronze mirrors that Corinth famously produced, which tended to distort and blur the image when they got old and dark. But you get the idea. A massive difference exists between seeing someone through a glass, darkly, and seeing them face to face. When you see someone through frosted glass, or in a dark and faded bronze mirror, you can work out their shape and the color of their clothes, but not their exact detail. You might be able to tell that a person is female and wearing a pink sleeveless top, but not that they have green eyes, mascara and dimples when they smile. For that, you would need to see them face to face.

This is how Paul describes the contrast between knowing Jesus now, and knowing him when he returns. For now, we see him in a limited fashion, through a glass darkly—enough to make out the shapes and colors and to give a general impression, but nothing like enough to give an accurate description. When Jesus comes back to reign, however, and renews the heavens and the earth, and gives resurrection bodies to all who love him, we will see him face to face, without any of these limitations and hindrances. We will know him fully, not just in part. Just think about that for a moment, because it has two wonderful implications.

Firstly, mystery is okay. If you're anything like me, you want answers to everything: the Trinity, sovereignty and freewill, suffering, and who killed JFK. But in many cases, we're not supposed to have all the answers—because we are looking through a glass darkly—and that's all right. We can make out shapes and colors of God's character and purposes, and he has revealed an awful lot of it, but it's never going to be as clear as we would like it to be. In fact, it's very good for us to have a sense of mystery when approaching the living God, and it certainly doesn't hurt us to shrug our shoulders every now and then, because it means we have to acknowledge our limitations.

The second implication is far more exciting, and it blows my mind. Even the most profound revelations of Jesus we have now are mere sketches, silhouettes, dim reflections of what he is actually like. That's incredible. I find Jesus a captivating and awe-inspiring person as it is, so the idea that I'm only seeing the Jesus of the Gospels, and even the Jesus of Revelation, "through a glass, darkly," is phenomenal—and it makes me wonder what on earth seeing him "face to face" will be like. If the love of the Jew from Nazareth is experienced through a glass darkly, what kind of love will we encounter when we see him face to face? If the power that stilled the storm is a misted image on a bronze plate, what will his power look like when we meet the real deal? And if people fell before him in delighted awe when the glass was opaque and frosted, what will we do when the glass is removed altogether? I can only imagine.

Yet that's where the stories are headed. Remember, Paul knew a fair bit about the revelation of Jesus; he knew his Old Testament backwards, then met the risen Jesus himself, then spent thirty years healing and preaching and raising the dead in Jesus' name. If anyone was entitled to think they had Jesus sorted, it was Paul. But the closer he got to Jesus, the bigger Jesus became, and the more Paul realized there was to know. So he looked forward to Jesus' return with all his being, while keeping a sense that he would never quite get his head round it.

So can we. We can celebrate the incomprehensible wonder of Jesus for now, yet with trembling excitement knowing we are only scratching the surface, like a couple who love being engaged but look forward to an even greater future. We can delight ourselves in the range and depth of his gospel stories, all the while suspecting, as C. S. Lewis put it, that we've only really got as far as the cover and the title page, and that the real story is yet to start. We can try to wrap our heads round the incomparable God and his unfathomable gospel—the story beneath the story and the gospel of the glory, shame removed and earth renewed, redemption and reconciliation—yet admit, with happy humility, that we really don't know what we're talking about. And we can preach stories with passion and joy, yet recognize that even on our best days we are looking at the one who wrote them through a frosted pane.

That's Jesus. The lion and the lamb, the lifeboat and the scapegoat. The star-forming, ocean-making, trespass-taking Lord of the world. And one day we will see him face to face:

> No longer will there be anything accursed, but the throne of God and of the Lamb will be in it, and his servants will worship him. They will see his face, and his name will be on their foreheads. And night will be no more. They will need no light of lamp or sun, for the Lord God will be their light, and they will reign forever and ever. (Revelation 22:3-5)

———

THE GOSPEL OF GOD

Now after John was arrested, Jesus
came into Galilee, proclaiming the
gospel of God.
(Mark 1:14)

Every story has a hero. And every gospel story has the same hero. Let's remind ourselves who he is.

He is the universe's creator, Adam and Eve's template, and the serpent's nemesis. He condemned Cain and accepted Abel. He was the destroyer of the earth in flood waters, but the rescuer of Noah and his family. He is the initiator of covenants, the inventor of the rainbow, the confuser of man's speech and the confounder of humanity's arrogance. He is Abraham's shield and his very great reward, the maker and keeper of outrageous promises, and the God who calls by grace and justifies by faith. He provides Isaac's substitute. He stands in the middle of Jacob's brook and at the top of Jacob's ladder, and turns a wheeler-dealer into the father of a nation.

He's the giver and fulfiller of Joseph's dreams, and the one who works for good what people had intended for evil, he saves a man, a family and an entire empire.

He is the God of the burning bush: Yahweh, I AM WHO I AM, the God of Israel. He is Moses' salvation, Aaron's inspiration, Miriam's celebration and Pharaoh's nightmare. It was he who destroyed Egypt with a river, healed Israel with a branch and crushed Amalek with a banner, so when he tells Israel they are to have no other gods but him, you had better take notice. He is in the cloud by day, the fire by night, the glory mist in the tent, the thunderstorm on the mountain, the water from the rock, the flame that consumes Nadab and Abihu, and the earthquake that swallows Korah. So unstoppable are his purposes that the rent-a-prophet Balaam is physically unable to speak against his people.

He is the commander of the army of Yahweh, producing the courage of Joshua, the refuge of Rahab, the parting of the Jordan and the collapse of Jericho. He is the song of Deborah, the sword of Gideon, and the strength of Samson. He opens Hannah's womb and Samuel's ears, and his ark alone—the box in which he lives—is enough to smash the Philistines, break their gods in pieces, win battles and conquer cities. He is David's rock, his shield, his fortress, his hiding place; yet he is also the forgiver of his sins and the restorer of his joy. To Solomon, he gives wisdom and wealth. To Elijah, he is the widow's oil, the Carmel fire and the still small voice. To Elisha, he makes the dead live, the leper clean and the axe-head float. He is Jehoshaphat's ambush, Hezekiah's deliverer, Sennacherib's conqueror, Josiah's lawgiver, Ezra's teacher, Nehemiah's confidence and

Esther's rescue. In other words, he is the hero of every story in the entire Old Testament.

And not just the stories. In Job, he is the truly sovereign one whose purposes are unsearchable and whose power is too wonderful to fathom. In one hundred and fifty psalms spanning a thousand years, he is the hope in every situation and the answer to every cry, not to mention the praise of every song. Marvelously, Isaiah's Holy One of Israel, Jeremiah's righteous branch, Ezekiel's Yahweh-who-is-there and Daniel's revealer of mysteries are all one and the same. Not only that, but the prophets then reveal God as Hosea's faithful Father, Joel's outpoured Spirit, Nahum's vengeant warrior, Jonah's merciful judge, Zephaniah's rejoicing husband and Zechariah's conquering king. By the time you finish Malachi, you cannot help but feel somewhat exhausted at the variety of the gospel stories and the majesty of their hero. The whole thing is, quite literally, the gospel of God.

Then a baby lets out his first cry. If you were impressed before, you can only stand amazed now, as the man from Nazareth embodies the story of God to perfection. The supporting cast reflect the brilliance of the hero by their remarkable range of reactions to him: overjoyed shepherds, a jealous king, a confused John the Baptizer, a loyal (but often even more confused) band of followers, exasperated Pharisees, overjoyed tax officials, furious temple leaders, welcomed prostitutes, frustrated militants, forgiven sinners. As God provides his clearest demonstration of what he is like, the human race is not sure what to make of him, but the stories continue. He is Nicodemus' answer, Legion's defeat, Lazarus' life, Caesar's alternative, Thomas' proof, and Peter's restoration. Finally, he is the defeat of sin and death, and in his crucifixion and resurrection he lays the foundation for the gospel of God to go global.

With the pouring out of the Holy Spirit, the stories multiply. Our hero appears all over the place. Luke's breathless account in Acts makes a valiant attempt to get it all down on paper—Barnabas' generosity, John's faith, Ananias' death, Stephen's conviction, Philip's evangelism, Paul's conversion, and the rest—but, like a six-year-old trying to get the football from Ronaldinho, Luke cannot keep up with the ever-expanding gospel stories that spring up from Antioch to Azotus, and ends his account with our hero still healing bodies and saving souls. As Acts finishes, the gospel of God is ongoing. And it still is.

So the whole Bible is about God. It is full of stories in which he is the main character, the climax, the resolution and indeed the author. The writers of Scripture were incapable of writing narratives, poems, prophecies or visions that weren't about God. In fact, so much is he the purpose, the hero and the punchline of all stories, that to talk about anything else would be to miss the point completely, like focusing on the frame of the Mona Lisa or the grass in front of the Taj Mahal. "For from him and through him and to him are all things. To him be glory forever. Amen" (Rom. 11:36).

Welcome to the gospel of God.

Acknowledgments

I am very grateful to Jonathan Carswell, Sheri Newton and everybody at 10ofThose for making possible this revision of my book *GodStories*. Particular thanks go to Lucy Samuel for her outstanding work on the new introduction, without which I might never have got this far; it was a privilege to work with you, Lucy. And my heartfelt gratitude goes to Judith Barnett, for fifteen years (and counting) of help, generosity, diligence, diplomacy, mischief, road trips, raspberries and overnight oats. Few people will ever know how much difference you've made to our lives, but hopefully you do.

More books from 10Publishing

Resources that point to Jesus